THE
PRINCE

THE
PRINCE

WITH STUDY GUIDE
BY THERESA PUSKAR

BY NICCOLO MACHIAVELLI

TRANSLATED BY
W. K. MARRIOTT

MEDIA

MEDIA

Published 2018 by Gildan Media LLC
aka G&D Media
www.GandDmedia.com

FIRST EDITION 2018

Front Cover design by David Rheinhardt of Pyrographx

Interior design by Meghan Day Healey of Story Horse, LLC

Library of Congress Cataloging-in-Publication Data is available upon request

ISBN: 978-1-7225-0008-5

10   9   8   7   6   5   4   3   2   1

Contents

Chapter I

Chapter II

Chapter III

Chapter IV

Chapter V

Chapter VI

Chapter VII

Chapter VIII

Chapter IX

Chapter X

Chapter XI

Chapter XII

Chapter XIII

Chapter XIV

Chapter XV

Chapter XVI

Chapter XVII

Chapter XVIII

Chapter XIX

Chapter XX

Chapter XXI

Chapter XXII

Chapter XXIII

Chapter XXIV

Chapter XXV

Chapter XXVI

*Niccolo Machiavelli was born at Florence
on 3rd May 1469. From 1494 to 1512 he held
an official post at Florence which included
diplomatic missions to various European courts.
Imprisoned in Florence, 1512; he was later
exiled and returned to San Casciano.*

He died at Florence on 22nd June 1527.

Foreword

Leading with Authentic Power

Study Guide on Machiavelli's The Prince

Throughout his lifetime and in the years that followed Niccolo Machiavelli was best known for his strategic thinking in the world of politics and power. His writings have remained timely and highly controversial. One of his more popular texts, **THE PRINCE** reflects on the failures and triumphs in the political standoffs, battles and strategic maneuverings that were played out among the leaders of European nations in his day. Without context, **THE PRINCE** can be a dense study. You would best be served by paying close attention to the strategies that he weaved throughout this treatise, as opposed to focusing on his commentaries about his contemporaries.

At times Machiavelli's messages can be extreme, suggesting violence and annihilation as options to gain power. While very contentious, he makes some poignant and powerful observations. Also, because his examinations are filled with historical references on the issues of the day, at first glance, they may not appear relevant. However, throughout the treatise he suggests a multitude of leadership practices and traits, as he shares insights on the victories and pitfalls made by the leaders of his day. With further reflection, you can gain a greater understanding of the inner workings of these leaders. Doing so sheds light on behaviors that can break failed leaders and those that can make great ones.

There are twenty-six chapters to **THE PRINCE**. Each chapter is followed by its Study Guide, providing a summary and insights on Machiavelli's teachings. Each chapter of the Study Guide, provides you with one of twenty-six fundamental traits that help to cultivate a successful leader. These traits are divided into three categories: Emotional, Physical and Intellectual Health.

Emotional Health—Internal Self

1. Drive—Passion and ability to step into the unknown
2. Proactivity—Ability to take immediate action
3. Faith—Ability to trust that things will work out
4. Vulnerability—Ability to be honest, humble and seen
5. Intuition—Ability to trust the voice from within
6. Focused—Ability to stay with a task or initiative

Emotional Health—External Self

7. Oratory—Ability to articulate ideas and initiatives
8. Grounded—Ability to stand rooted, firm and strong
9. Non-Reactive—Ability to take criticism impersonally

10. Objective—Ability to see reality beyond internal struggles
11. Attentive—Ability to actively listen
12. Charismatic—Ability to draw people to follow you
13. Recruiter—Ability to see and seek talent in others

Physical health

14. Strength—Ability to keep physical body strong to support mental
15. Endurance—Ability to remain energized for prolonged periods of time
16. Flexibility—Ability to be malleable and be open to change
17. Balance—Ability to maintain equilibrium
18. Nourishment—Ability to absorb energetic nourishment

Intellectual health

19. Inspiration—Ability to stir the souls of your followers
20. Strategic thinking—Ability to see the big picture and think ahead
21. Loyalty—Ability to stand by others through thick and thin
22. Economy—Ability to achieve much with little
23. Decisiveness—Ability to make immediate decisions
24. Vision—Ability to see possibilities
25. Operational—Ability to see big picture
26. Confidence—Ability to honor yourself whatever the outcome

Should you wish to gain and maintain authentic power, you would be wise to master each of these traits. Building upon the suggestions outlined in this manual can assist you in avoiding the trappings under which many of the failed leaders Machiavelli references in his treatise have fallen prey. Whether your battles are in the boardroom, in the living room or within your own mind, reflecting on Machiavelli's potent teachings along with cultivating the skills listed above will provide you with a greater understanding of how the wheel of power turns, and how you may triumph as a key cog in that wheel.

Theresa Puskar
Study Guide Author

Introduction

Machiavelli's The Prince

Niccolo Machiavelli was born in Florence on 3rd May 1469. He was the second son of Bernardo di Niccolo Machiavelli, a lawyer of some repute, and of Bartolomea di Stefano Nelli, his wife. Both parents were members of the old Florentine nobility.

His life falls naturally into three periods, each of which singularly enough constitutes a distinct and important era in the history of Florence. His youth was concurrent with the greatness of Florence as an Italian power under the guidance of Lorenzo de' Medici, Il Magnifico. The downfall of the Medici in Florence occurred in 1494, in which year Machiavelli entered the public service. During his official career Florence was free under the government of a Republic, which lasted until 1512, when the Medici returned to power, and Machiavelli lost his office. The Medici again ruled Florence from 1512 until 1527, when they were once more driven out. This was the period of Machiavelli's literary activity and increasing influence; but he died, within a few weeks of the expulsion of the Medici, on 22nd June 1527, in his fifty-eighth year, without having regained office.

Youth • 1469–1494
Ages 1–25

Although there is little recorded of the youth of Machiavelli, the Florence of those days is so well known that the early environment of this representative citizen may be easily imagined. Florence has been described as a city with two opposite currents of life, one directed by the fervent and austere Savonarola, the other by the splendor-loving Lorenzo. Savonarola's influence upon the young Machiavelli must have been slight, for although at one time he wielded immense power over the fortunes of Florence, he only furnished Machiavelli with a subject of a gibe in THE PRINCE where he is cited as an example of an unarmed prophet who came to a bad end. Whereas the magnificence of the Medicean rule during the life of Lorenzo appeared to have impressed Machiavelli strongly, for he frequently recurs to it in his writings and it is to Lorenzo's grandson that he dedicates THE PRINCE.

Machiavelli, in his HISTORY OF FLORENCE, gives us a picture of the young men among whom his youth was passed. He writes: "They were freer than their forefathers in dress and living, and spent more in other kinds of excesses, consuming their time and money in idleness, gaming, and women; their chief aim was to appear well dressed and to speak with wit and acuteness, whilst he who could wound others the most cleverly was thought the wisest." In a letter to his son Guido, Machiavelli shows why youth should avail itself of its opportunities for study, and leads us to infer that his own youth had been so occupied. He writes: "I have received your letter, which has given me the greatest pleasure, especially because you tell me you are quite restored in health, than which I could have no better news; for if God grant life to you, and to me, I hope to make a good man of you if you are willing to do your share." Then, writing of a new patron, he continues: "This will turn out well for you, but it is necessary for you to study; since, then, you have no longer the excuse of illness, take pains to study letters and music, for you see what honor is done to me for the little skill I have.

Therefore, my son, if you wish to please me, and to bring success and honor to yourself, do right and study, because others will help you if you help yourself."

Office • 1494–1512
Ages 25–43

The second period of Machiavelli's life was spent in the service of the free Republic of Florence, which flourished, as stated above, from the expulsion of the Medici in 1494 until their return in 1512. After serving four years in one of the public offices he was appointed Chancellor and Secretary to the Second Chancery, the Ten of Liberty and Peace. Here we are on firm ground when dealing with the events of Machiavelli's life, for during this time he took a leading part in the affairs of the Republic, and we have its decrees, records, and dispatches to guide us, as well as his own writings. A mere recapitulation of a few of his transactions with the statesmen and soldiers of his time gives a fair indication of his activities, and supplies the sources from which he drew the experiences and characters which illustrate **THE PRINCE**.

His first mission was in 1499 to Catherina Sforza, "my lady of Forli" of **THE PRINCE**," from whose conduct and fate he drew the moral that it is far better to earn the confidence of the people than to rely on fortresses. This is a very noticeable principle in Machiavelli, and is urged by him in many ways as a matter of vital importance to princes.

In 1500 he was sent to France to obtain terms from Louis XII for continuing the war against Pisa: this king it was who, in his conduct of affairs in Italy, committed the five capital errors in statecraft summarized in **THE PRINCE** and was consequently driven out.

He, also, it was who made the dissolution of his marriage a condition of support to Pope Alexander VI; which leads Machiavelli to refer those who urge that such promises should be kept to what he has written concerning the faith of princes.

Machiavelli's public life was largely occupied with events arising out of the ambitions of Pope Alexander VI and his son, Cesare Borgia, the Duke Valentino, and these characters fill a large space of **THE PRINCE**. Machiavelli never hesitates to cite the actions of the duke for the benefit of usurpers who wish to keep the states they have seized; he can, indeed, find no precepts to offer so good as the pattern of Cesare Borgia's conduct, insomuch that Cesare is acclaimed by some critics as the "hero" of **THE PRINCE**. Yet in **THE PRINCE** the duke is in point of fact cited as a type of the man who rises on the fortune of others, and falls with them; who takes every course that might be expected from a prudent man but the course which will save him; who is prepared for all eventualities but the one which happens; and who, when all his abilities fail to carry him through, exclaims that it was not his fault, but an extraordinary and unforeseen fatality.

On the death of Pius III, in 1503, Machiavelli was sent to Rome to watch the election of his successor, and there he saw Cesare Borgia cheated into allowing the choice of the College to fall on Giuliano delle Rovere (Julius II), who was one of the cardinals that had most reason to fear the duke. Machiavelli, when commenting on this election, says that he who thinks new favors will cause great personages to forget old injuries deceives himself. Julius did not rest until he had ruined Cesare.

It was to Julius II that Machiavelli was sent in 1506, when that pontiff was commencing his enterprise against Bologna; which he brought to a successful issue, as he did many of his other adventures, owing chiefly to his impetuous character. It is in reference to Pope Julius that Machiavelli moralizes on the resemblance between Fortune and women, and concludes that it is the bold rather than the cautious man that will win and hold them both.

It is impossible to follow here the varying fortunes of the Italian states, which in 1507 were controlled by France, Spain, and Germany, with results that have lasted to our day; we are concerned with those events, and with the three great actors in them, so far only as they impinge on the personality of Machiavelli. He had several meetings with Louis XII of France, and his estimate of that monarch's character has already been alluded to. Machiavelli has painted Ferdinand of Aragon as the man who accomplished great things under the cloak of religion,but who in reality had no mercy, faith, humanity, or integrity; and who, had he allowed himself to be influenced by such motives, would have been ruined. The Emperor Maximilian was one of the most interesting men of the age, and his character has been drawn by many hands; but Machiavelli, who was an envoy at his court in 1507-8, reveals the secret of his many failures when he describes him as a secretive man, without force of character—ignoring the human agencies necessary to carry his schemes into effect, and never insisting on the fulfilment of his wishes.

The remaining years of Machiavelli's official career were filled with events arising out of the League of Cambrai, made in 1508 between the three great European powers already mentioned and the Pope, with the object of crushing the Venetian Republic. This result was attained in the battle of Vaila, when Venice lost in one day all that she had won in eight hundred years. Florence had a difficult part to play during these events, complicated as they were by the feud which broke out between the Pope and the French, because friendship with France had dictated the entire policy of the Republic. When, in 1511, Julius II finally formed the Holy League against France, and with the assistance of the Swiss drove the French out of Italy, Florence lay at the mercy of the Pope, and had to submit to his terms, one of which was that the Medici should be restored. The return of the Medici to Florence on 1st September 1512, and the consequent fall of the Republic, was the signal for the dismissal of Machiavelli and his friends, and thus put an end to his public career, for, as we have seen, he died without regaining office.

Literature and Death • 1512–1527
Ages 43–58

On the return of the Medici, Machiavelli, who for a few weeks had vainly hoped to retain his office under the new masters of Florence, was dismissed by decree dated 7th November 1512. Shortly after this he was accused of complicity in an abortive conspiracy against the Medici, imprisoned, and put to the question by torture. The new Medicean Pope, Leo X, procured his release, and he retired to his small property at San Casciano, near Florence, where he devoted himself to literature. In a letter to Francesco Vettori, dated 13th December 1513, he has left a very interesting description of his life at this period, which elucidates his methods and his motives in writing **THE PRINCE**. After describing his daily occupations with his family and neighbors, he writes: "The evening being come, I return home and go to my study; at the entrance I pull off my peasant-clothes, covered with dust and dirt, and put on my noble court dress, and thus becomingly re-clothed I pass into the ancient courts of the men of old, where, being lovingly received by them, I am fed with that food which is mine alone; where I do not hesitate to speak with them, and to ask for the reason of their actions, and they in their benignity answer me; and for four hours I feel no weariness, I forget every trouble, poverty does not dismay, death does not terrify me; I am possessed entirely by those great men. And because Dante says:

> *Knowledge doth come of learning well retained,*
> *Unfruitful else,*

I have noted down what I have gained from their conversation, and have composed a small work on 'Principalities,' where I pour myself out as fully as I can in meditation on the subject, discussing what a principality is, what kinds there are, how they can be acquired, how they can be kept, why they are lost: and if any of my fancies ever pleased you, this ought not to displease you: and to a prince, especially to a new one, it should be welcome: therefore I dedicate it to his Magnificence Giuliano. Filippo Casavecchia has seen it; he will be able to tell you what is in it, and of the discourses I have had with him; nevertheless, I am still enriching and polishing it."

The "little book" suffered many vicissitudes before attaining the form in which it has reached us. Various mental influences were at work during its composition; its title and patron were changed; and for some unknown reason it was finally dedicated to Lorenzo de' Medici. Although Machiavelli discussed with Casavecchia whether it should be sent or presented in person to the patron, there is no evidence that Lorenzo ever received or even read it: he certainly never gave Machiavelli any employment. Although it was plagiarized during Machiavelli's lifetime, THE PRINCE was never published by him, and its text is still disputable.

Machiavelli concludes his letter to Vettori thus: "And as to this little thing [his book], when it has been read it will be seen that during the fifteen years I have given to the study of statecraft I have neither slept nor idled; and men ought ever to desire to be served by one who has reaped experience at the expense of others. And of my loyalty none could doubt, because having always kept faith I could not now learn how to break it; for he who has been faithful and honest, as I have, cannot change his nature; and my poverty is a witness to my honesty."

Before Machiavelli had got THE PRINCE off his hands he commenced his DISCOURSE ON THE FIRST DECADE OF TITUS LIVIUS, which should be read concurrently with THE PRINCE. These and several minor works occupied him until the year 1518, when he accepted a small commission to look after the affairs of some Florentine merchants at Genoa. In 1519 the Medicean rulers of Florence granted a few political concessions to her citizens, and Machiavelli with others was consulted upon a new constitution under which the Great Council was to be restored; but on one pretext or another it was not promulgated.

In 1520 the Florentine merchants again had recourse to Machiavelli to settle their difficulties with Lucca, but this year was chiefly remarkable for his re-entry into Florentine literary society, where he was much sought after, and also for the production of his **ART OF WAR**. It was in the same year that he received a commission at the instance of Cardinal de' Medici to write the **HISTORY OF FLORENCE**, a task which occupied him until 1525. His return to popular favor may have determined the Medici to give him this employment, for an old writer observes that "an able statesman out of work, like a huge whale, will endeavor to overturn the ship unless he has an empty cask to play with."

When the **HISTORY OF FLORENCE** was finished, Machiavelli took it to Rome for presentation to his patron, Giuliano de' Medici, who had in the meanwhile become Pope under the title of Clement VII. It is somewhat remarkable that, as, in 1513, Machiavelli had written **THE PRINCE** for the instruction of the Medici after they had just regained power in Florence, so, in 1525, he dedicated the **HISTORY OF FLORENCE** to the head of the family when its ruin was now at hand. In that year the battle of Pavia destroyed the French rule in Italy, and left Francis I a prisoner in the hands of his great rival, Charles V. This was followed by the sack of Rome, upon the news of which the popular party at Florence threw off the yoke of the Medici, who were once more banished.

Machiavelli was absent from Florence at this time, but hastened his return, hoping to secure his former office of secretary to the "Ten of Liberty and Peace." Unhappily he was taken ill soon after he reached Florence, where he died on 22nd June 1527.

The Man and His Works

No one can say where the bones of Machiavelli rest, but modern Florence has decreed him a stately cenotaph in Santa Croce, by the side of her most famous sons; recognizing that, whatever other nations may have found in his works, Italy found in them the idea of her unity and the germs of her renaissance among the nations of Europe. Whilst it is idle to protest against the world-wide and evil signification of his name, it may be pointed out that the harsh construction of his doctrine which this sinister reputation implies was unknown to his own day, and that the researches of recent times have enabled us to interpret him more reasonably. It is due to these inquiries that the shape of an "unholy necromancer," which so long haunted men's vision, has begun to fade.

Machiavelli was undoubtedly a man of great observation, acuteness, and industry; noting with appreciative eye whatever passed before him, and with his supreme literary gift turning it to account in his enforced retirement from affairs. He does not present himself, nor is he depicted by his contemporaries, as a type of that rare combination, the successful statesman and author, for he appears to have been only moderately prosperous in his several embassies and political employments. He was misled by Catherina Sforza, ignored by Louis XII, overawed by Cesare Borgia; several of his embassies were quite barren of results; his attempts to fortify Florence failed, and the soldiery that he raised astonished everybody by their cowardice. In the conduct of his own affairs he was timid and time-serving; he dared not appear by the side of Soderini, to whom he owed so much, for fear of compromising himself; his connection with the Medici was open to suspicion, and Giuliano appears to have recognized his real forte when he set him to write the **HISTORY OF FLORENCE** rather than employ him in the state.

And it is on the literary side of his character, and there alone, that we find no weakness and no failure.

Although the light of almost four centuries has been focused on **THE PRINCE**, its problems are still debatable and interesting, because they are the eternal problems between the ruled and their rulers. Such as they are, its ethics are those of Machiavelli's contemporaries; yet they cannot be said to be out of date so long as the governments of Europe rely on material rather than on moral forces. Its historical incidents and personages become interesting by reason of the uses which Machiavelli makes of them to illustrate his theories of government and conduct.

Leaving out of consideration those maxims of state which still furnish some European and eastern statesmen with principles of action, **THE PRINCE** is bestrewn with truths that can be proved at every turn. Men are still the dupes of their simplicity and greed, as they were in the days of Alexander VI. The cloak of religion still conceals the vices which Machiavelli laid bare in the character of Ferdinand of Aragon. Men will not look at things as they really are, but as they wish them to be—and are ruined. In politics there are no perfectly safe courses;

prudence consists in choosing the least dangerous ones. Then—to pass to a higher plane—Machiavelli reiterates that, although crimes may win an empire, they do not win glory. Necessary wars are just wars, and the arms of a nation are hallowed when it has no other resource but to fight.

It is the cry of a far later day than Machiavelli's that government should be elevated into a living moral force, capable of inspiring the people with a just recognition of the fundamental principles of society; to this "high argument" THE PRINCE contributes but little. Machiavelli always refused to write either of men or of governments otherwise than as he found them, and he writes with such skill and insight that his work is of abiding value. But what invests THE PRINCE with more than a merely artistic or historical interest is the incontrovertible truth that it deals with the great principles which still guide nations and rulers in their relationship with each other and their neighbors.

In translating THE PRINCE my aim has been to achieve at all costs an exact literal rendering of the original, rather than a fluent paraphrase adapted to the modern notions of style and expression. Machiavelli was no facile phrasemonger; the conditions under which he wrote obliged him to weigh every word; his themes were lofty, his substance grave, his manner nobly plain and serious. "Quis eo fuit unquam in partiundis rebus, in definiendis, in explanandis pressior?" In THE PRINCE it may be truly said, there is reason assignable, not only for every word, but for the position of every word. To an Englishman of Shakespeare's time the translation of such a treatise was in some ways a comparatively easy task, for in those times the genius of the English more nearly resembled that of the Italian language; to the Englishman of to-day it is not so simple. To take a single example: the word "intrattenere," employed by Machiavelli to indicate the policy adopted by the Roman Senate towards the weaker states of Greece, would by an Elizabethan be correctly rendered "entertain," and every contemporary reader would understand what was meant by saying that "Rome entertained the Aetolians and the Achaeans without augmenting their power." But today such a phrase would seem obsolete and ambiguous, if not unmeaning: we are compelled to say that "Rome maintained friendly relations with the Aetolians," etc., using four words to do the work of one. I have tried to preserve the pithy brevity of the Italian so far as was consistent with an absolute fidelity to the sense. If the result be an occasional asperity I can only hope that the reader, in his eagerness to reach the author's meaning, may overlook the roughness of the road that leads him to it.

The following is a list of the works of Machiavelli:

Principal works. Discorso sopra le cose di Pisa, 1499; Del modo di trattare i popoli della Valdichiana ribellati, 1502; Del modo tenuto dal duca Valentino nell' ammazzare Vitellozzo Vitelli, Oliverotto da Fermo, etc., 1502; Discorso sopra la provisione del danaro, 1502; Decennale primo (poem in terza rima), 1506; Ritratti delle cose dell' Alemagna, 1508-12; Decennale secondo, 1509; Ritratti delle cose di Francia, 1510; Discorsi sopra la prima deca di T. Livio, 3 vols., 1512- 17; Il Principe, 1513; Andria, comedy translated from Terence, 1513 (?); Mandragola, prose comedy in five acts, with prologue in verse, 1513; Della lingua (dialogue), 1514; Clizia, comedy in prose, 1515 (?); Belfagor arcidiavolo (novel), 1515; Asino d'oro (poem in terza rima), 1517; Dell' arte della guerra, 1519-20; Discorso sopra il riformare lo stato di Firenze, 1520; Sommario delle cose della citta di Lucca, 1520; Vita di Castruccio Castracani da Lucca, 1520; Istorie fiorentine, 8 books, 1521-5; Frammenti storici, 1525.

Other poems include Sonetti, Canzoni, Ottave, and Canti carnascialeschi.

Editions. Aldo, Venice, 1546; della Tertina, 1550; Cambiagi, Florence, 6 vols., 1782-5; dei Classici, Milan, 10 1813; Silvestri, 9 vols., 1820-2; Passerini, Fanfani, Milanesi, 6 vols. only published, 1873-7.

Minor works. Ed. F. L. Polidori, 1852; Lettere familiari, ed. E. Alvisi, 1883, 2 editions, one with excisions; Credited Writings, ed. G. Canestrini, 1857; Letters to Vettori, see A. Ridolfi, Pensieri intorno allo scopo di N. Machiavelli nel libro Il Principe, etc.; D. Ferrara, The Private Correspondence of Niccolo Machiavelli, 1929.

STUDY GUIDE

Introduction

Power can be precarious. One can be at the top of their game in one moment, and fall to their peril the next. The question remains, *"How does one gain power, and then how can he or she maintain it?"* We each harbor opinions and beliefs about power—many of them unconscious. Before you can achieve true authentic power, you need to reflect on those opinions so that you can be aware of them. Only from a place of awareness can you change them. In this manual we will clarify what *authentic* power is, and then using Machiavelli's treatise as a reference point, we will share insights, tools and practical techniques you can use to build your own authenticity-based power structure.

Machiavelli was born in 1469. Constructed below is a timeline to provide you with the context by which he views that time in history.

1469–1494	1494–1512	1512–1527
YOUTH	TIME IN OFFICE	WRITING/DEATH
(1494 Downfall of L.de'Medici)		*(1512 de' Medici Rise)*

1. Niccolo Machiavelli lived a full and hearty life. As is evident in his biography at the beginning of the book, as well as being a political strategist, he held several positions in public office, was a successful playwright, and an outspoken and esteemed literary commentator on the

politics and power plays of his era. Write a list of your accomplishments.

2. Write of list of undertakings that you have not mastered, but you would like to add to the list you created above.

3. In the text, Machiavelli was noted as being *"a man of great observation, acuteness, and industry."* He was noted for being strongly opinionated and at times ruthless in his initiatives on how to gain power. Some of his critics thought that in this text he blatantly encouraged violent and corrupt behavior in order to gain power. There is a famous saying that *"power corrupts."* Take a few moments and reflect on this statement. What are your views on power and corruption? Do you believe that power corrupts?

4. To further clarify your perspective, define what constitutes "corruption."

5. Write a list of powerful individuals throughout history that you believe have used corruption in gaining their power.

6. Do you harbor any fears that you could become corrupt if you gained great power? Write about your fears or lack thereof.

7. Are there any parameters that you could put in place that would call you to task should you display corrupt behavior as you seek to gain power in your life? If so, what are they? If not, want checks and balances can you put in place?

8. One may classify power in two distinct categories. The first of these is pseudo power. Pseudo-power exists when the leader governs from a place of aggression. The system that they have created to support their power is fear-based. Their subordinates do not follow them out

of reverence and respect, but from a state of anxiety and trepidation. This happens when the leader governs through bullying, manipulation and force. While individuals under their reign may obey, their hearts are not at all in sync with their leader. Write a list of individual that you know (personally, or in history) who have possessed pseudo-power, leading through fear and intimidation.

9. Reflect on your life. Have you ever lead others through aggression? You may have small or large examples of this in your life. One example maybe as slight as name-calling, or threatening a fellow child when you were young. You may have more blatant situations where you placed yourself above a friend or colleague, and intimidated them when they voiced an opinion that differed from yours. List any situations in which you believe you were a bully in your life.

10. If you found examples of times when you were a bully in pseudo-power, what was the outcome of your efforts? Did the situation ultimately work out in your favor?

11. Reflect even deeper in these situations, and ask yourself why you bullied. Most often you will find that your own fear was at the root of your behavior. You may not have believed that you deserved to be in power, or feared that others would follow you if you were not aggressive. Write about any insight you have on this.

12. The second kind of leader is the individual who leads from a place of authentic power. He or she governs from a place of confidence, gaining the love, loyalty and respect of his/her subordinates through integrity and wisdom-based initiatives. Reflect on this and write a list of such leaders.

13. Beside the names of the individual that you just referenced above, list the traits that each possessed which made them so remarkable.

14. Which of these traits do you currently possess?

15. Which of these traits would you like to further cultivate in yourself?

16. What small action step(s) can you currently take to begin developing this trait within you?

Dedication for The Prince

To the Magnificent Lorenzo Di Piero De' Medici:

*Those who strive to obtain the good graces of a prince
are accustomed to come before him with such things as
they hold most precious, or in which they see him take
most delight; whence one often sees horses, arms, cloth
of gold, precious stones, and similar ornaments presented
to princes, worthy of their greatness.*

*Desiring therefore to present myself to your Magnificence
with some testimony of my devotion towards you, I have
not found among my possessions anything which I hold
more dear than, or value so much as, the knowledge of
the actions of great men, acquired by long experience
in contemporary affairs, and a continual study of
antiquity; which, having reflected upon it with great
and prolonged diligence, I now send, digested into a
little volume, to your Magnificence.*

*And although I may consider this work unworthy of
your countenance, nevertheless I trust much to your
benignity that it may be acceptable, seeing that it is not
possible for me to make a better gift than to offer you the
opportunity of understanding in the shortest time all*

that I have learnt in so many years, and with so many troubles and dangers; which work I have not embellished with swelling or magnificent words, nor stuffed with rounded periods, nor with any extrinsic allurements or adornments whatever, with which so many are accustomed to embellish their works; for I have wished either that no honor should be given it, or else that the truth of the matter and the weightiness of the theme shall make it acceptable.

Nor do I hold with those who regard it as a presumption if a man of low and humble condition dare to discuss and settle the concerns of princes; because, just as those who draw landscapes place themselves below in the plain to contemplate the nature of the mountains and of lofty places, and in order to contemplate the plains place themselves upon high mountains, even so to understand the nature of the people it needs to be a prince, and to understand that of princes it needs to be of the people.

Take then, your Magnificence, this little gift in the spirit in which I send it; wherein, if it be diligently read and considered by you, you will learn my extreme desire that you should attain that greatness which fortune and your other attributes promise. And if your Magnificence from the summit of your greatness will sometimes turn your eyes to these lower regions, you will see how unmeritedly I suffer a great and continued malignity of fortune.

STUDY GUIDE

Dedication for The Prince

1. In his dedication to Lorenzo Di Piero De' Medici, Machiavelli states, *"I have not found among my possessions anything which I hold more dear than, or value so much as, the knowledge of the actions of great men . . ."* On a scale from one to ten, rate how much value you place on political or social leadership (one being "not at all important" and ten being "of great significance tome").

1———2———3———4———5———6———7———8———9———10

2. After reading Machiavelli's dedication, write your own dedication to someone that you greatly admire and respect (this does not have to be someone you personally know. It may be a public figure.)

Chapter I

How Many Kinds of Principalities There Are and By What Means They Are Acquired

All states, all powers, that have held and hold rule over men have been and are either republics or principalities. Principalities are either hereditary, in which the family has been long established; or they are new.

The new are either entirely new, as was Milan to Francesco Sforza, or they are, as it were, members annexed to the hereditary state of the prince who has acquired them, as was the kingdom of Naples to that of the King of Spain.

Such dominions thus acquired are either accustomed to live under a prince, or to live in freedom; and are acquired either by the arms of the prince himself, or of others, or else by fortune or by ability.

All states are: Republics or Principalities (hereditary or new)

STUDY GUIDE

Chapter I

Leadership Trait #1
Passion—
Drive and the Ability to Step into the Unknown

In this chapter Machiavelli shares information and insights on how power and leadership are gained. He references two states: Republics and Principalities. In the case of Principalities, they are either sought after through cunning and strategy or inherited. In order to learn about what will or will not work for you as you seek greater power and strength in your leadership initiatives, it is important that you understand what your current beliefs are and whether they help or hinder you. In this chapter you are going to decipher what your beliefs and expectations are around leadership, and how they do or do not serve you.

The leadership trait you will be focusing on in this chapter is *passion—drive and the ability to step into the unknown.* While many have dreams that they wish to pursue, few possess the passion and subsequent drive to manifest them in their lives. To be an effective leader, you must have a vision and then cultivate the knowledge, support and circumstances to bring it to fruition.

1. Machiavelli opens this chapter stating that all states are one of two things: Republics or Principalities. Principalities are either new or inherited. What are your beliefs

around wealth that has been inherited versus wealth that has been acquired through hard work? Do you believe that one who receives wealth and power due to lineage is deserving of it? Why or why not?

2. On a scale from one to ten (one being "not at all" and ten being"very much so"), rate how worthy do you believe you are of being wealthy:

1——2——3——4——5——6——7——8——9——10

3. Are there any reasons why you don't believe you deserve wealth? If so, what are they?

4. If you believe you are deserving of wealth, why do you think you have not yet attained it (if you have, how did you do so?)

5. Do you have any fears around being wealthy? If you are aware of any, what are they?

6. On a scale from one to ten (one being "not at all" and ten being"very much so"), rate how worthy you believe you are of being powerful:

1——2——3——4——5——6——7——8——9——10

7. Are there any reasons why you don't believe you deserve power? If so, what are they?

8. If you believe you are deserving of power, why do you think you have not yet attained it (if you have, how did you do so?

9. Do you have any fears around acquiring power? If so, what are they?

10. Do you believe you may have blocks or prejudices around easy acquisition of wealth and power? In other words, do you hold a belief that you need to work hard in order to

succeed? Write about your belief system and how it does or doesn't serve you.

11. The leadership trait you will be focusing on in this chapter is *passion—drive and the ability to step into the unknown.* On a scale from one to ten (one being "not at all" and ten being "very much so"), rate how passionate you are about your leadership initiatives:

12. Write a passionate description of what your leadership goals are.

13. Take your description, and write an elevator speech that condenses your description into one or two sentences.

14. Your elevator speech should be provocative and engaging. Read it to a couple of people. Get feedback as to whether they were moved and excited by it. Tweak it if necessary.

15. While passion is powerful, action is essential. On a scale from one to ten (one being "not at all" and ten being "very much so"), rate how driven you are towards manifesting your leadership goals:

16. Are there any areas in your initiative where you lack drive? For example, some individuals love to envision, but do not like to build their vision into fruition. Others love to create, but perhaps are not successful marketers. List the areas that you see as challenging.

17. Ideally, if you are not passionate about particular areas of your initiative, you may require assistance from others. Go through the list you created in #16. Are there individuals you could recruit to follow through in the areas of you

endeavor where you lack passion? List the positions and the potentials individuals you could recruit.

18. Do you have any fear around stepping into the unknown? Explain.

19. What steps could you take to alleviate your fears if you have any?

Chapter II

Concerning Hereditary Principalities

I will leave out all discussion on republics, inasmuch as in another place I have written of them at length, and will address myself only to principalities. In doing so I will keep to the order indicated above, and discuss how such principalities are to be ruled and preserved.

I say at once there are fewer difficulties in holding hereditary states, and those long accustomed to the family of their prince, than new ones; for it is sufficient only not to transgress the customs of his ancestors, and to deal prudently with circumstances as they arise, for a prince of average powers to maintain himself in his state, unless he be deprived of it by some extraordinary and excessive force; and if he should be so deprived of it, whenever anything sinister happens to the usurper, he will regain it.

We have in Italy, for example, the Duke of Ferrara, who could not have withstood the attacks of the Venetians in '84, nor those of Pope Julius in '10, unless he had been long established in his dominions. For the hereditary prince has less cause and less necessity to offend;

hence it happens that he will be more loved; and unless extraordinary vices cause him to be hated, it is reasonable to expect that his subjects will be naturally well disposed towards him; and in the antiquity and duration of his rule the memories and motives that make for change are lost, for one change always leaves the toothing for another.

Inheriting leadership is easier because you have picked up where family left behind. Without having to fight for your domain, being popular and loved is easy.

STUDY GUIDE

Chapter II

Leadership Trait #2
Proactive—Ability to Take Immediate Action

Machiavelli shares insights on inherited leaderships and their inherent challenges in this chapter. While it appears to be easy, this is not always the case. This raises the question as to whether one's lot in life is somewhat random or influenced more by events as they arise, or pre-destined. In this segment of the study guide, you are going to explore what your beliefs are around "destiny" as well as how character traits (whether inherited or not) play a part in your past, present and current leadership initiatives.

The leadership trait affiliated with this chapter is *proactivity—the ability to take immediate action*. Many people are visionaries, but lack the ability to move on their insights and ideas. Vision without action is futile. Being proactive and taking initiative is key in becoming a successful leader.

1. In this chapter the author states that inheriting a leadership position is easy because you have picked up what family left behind. Without having to fight for your domain, being popular and loved is easy. Do you believe your life is pre-determined; that your lot in life has been set? Do you believe that you have control over what happens to you?

2. If you believe that your life has been pre-determined, then what action steps can you take to empower yourself and move towards achieving your goals?

3. If you believe that you have control over what happens in your life, then list what specific steps you are currently taking to further develop your leadership skills.

4. Write a list of the traits that you have inherited from your lineage. To do so, create two columns. In the first column list all of those traits that you believe to be positive. In the second column list all of those traits that you believe to be negative.

5. Now circle in red the traits within each column that you believe will support you in your leadership initiatives.

6. Circle in blue those traits that you believe keep you from achieving your goals as a successful leader.

7. Based on this list, write down at least three action steps that you can take to further develop your character as a leader.

8. The leadership trait affiliated with this chapter is *proactivity— the ability to take immediate action*. On a scale from one to ten (one being "not at all" and ten being "very much so"), rate how often you procrastinate when dealing with a difficult decision or situation.

1———2———3———4———5———6———7———8———9———10

9. When you reflect on the times that you have procrastinated, why did you do so? Was there something or someone that you feared?

10. What was the outcome when you procrastinated?

11. It is important that a leader foresees potential issues, and addresses them before they become obvious. Time can work in your favor if you are aware and proactive. On a scale from one to ten (one being not very, and ten being extremely), rate how proactive you are.

1——2——3——4——5——6——7——8——9——10

12. It is said that when you have a new idea, at least two others are having it at the same time. Victory is most often celebrated by the individual who is the initiate in the game—the one who takes immediate action. Note any situations in which you had an idea, but didn't follow it through. Did you later discover than someone else did take action? If so, what was the outcome?

13. What three steps can you take to become more proactive, taking immediate action when necessary?

Chapter III

Concerning Mixed Principalities

But the difficulties occur in a new principality. And firstly, if it be not entirely new, but is, as it were, a member of a state which, taken collectively, may be called composite, the changes arise chiefly from an inherent difficulty which there is in all new principalities; for men change their rulers willingly, hoping to better themselves, and this hope induces them to take up arms against him who rules: wherein they are deceived, because they afterwards find by experience they have gone from bad to worse. This follows also on another natural and common necessity, which always causes a new prince to burden those who have submitted to him with his soldiery and with infinite other hardships which he must put upon his new acquisition.

Difficulties occur in new principalities (new domain). Men often change their leaders in hopes of finding someone better, but in the end, things are usually not improved upon. New leaders must thus burden those who support him with his soldiery (imposing force and might over them to instill trust, a firm rooting of himself.)

In this way you have enemies in all those whom you have injured in seizing that principality,and you are not able to keep those friends who put you there because of your not being able to satisfy them in the way they expected, and you cannot take strong measures against them, feeling bound to them. For, although one may be very strong in armed forces, yet in entering a province one has always need of the goodwill of the natives.

The leader ends up unable to please anyone. You injury enemies in seizing your power, and you feel bound to friends. You need the goodwill and support of the masses—not fighting and force.

For these reasons Louis the Twelfth, King of France, quickly occupied Milan, and as quickly lost it; and to turn him out the first time it only needed Lodovico's own forces; because those who had opened the gates to him, finding themselves deceived in their hopes of future benefit, would not endure the ill-treatment of the new prince. It is very true that, after acquiring rebellious provinces a second time, they are not so lightly lost afterwards, because the prince, with little reluctance, takes the opportunity of the rebellion to punish the delinquents, to clear out the suspects, and to strengthen himself in the weakest places. Thus to cause France to lose Milan the first time it was enough for the Duke Lodovico* to raise insurrections on the borders; but to cause him to lose it

---

* Duke Lodovico was Lodovico Moro, a son of Francesco Sforza, who married Beatrice d'Este. He ruled over Milan from 1494 to 1500, and died in 1510.

a second time it was necessary to bring the whole world against him, and that his armies should be defeated and driven out of Italy; which followed from the causes above mentioned.

Louis XII, King of France tried to take over leadership of Milan and lost because he treated the reigning prince poorly. Their hopes and dreams had been instilled in the Prince. He used the overthrow attempt as an opportunity to rid the land of negativity, and suspects—strengthening himself where there was weakness.

Nevertheless Milan was taken from France both the first and the second time. The general reasons for the first have been discussed; it remains to name those for the second, and to see what resources he had, and what any one in his situation would have had for maintaining himself more securely in his acquisition than did the King of France.

Now I say that those dominions which, when acquired, are added to an ancient state by him who acquires them, are either of the same country and language, or they are not. When they are, it is easier to hold them, especially when they have not been accustomed to self-government; and to hold them securely it is enough to have destroyed the family of the prince who was ruling them; because the two peoples, preserving in other things the old conditions, and not being unlike in customs, will live quietly together, as one has seen in Brittany, Burgundy, Gascony, and Normandy, which have been bound to France for so long a time: and, although there may be some difference in language, nevertheless the customs are alike, and the people will easily be able to get on amongst themselves. He who has annexed them, if he wishes to hold them, has only to bear in mind two considerations: the one, that the family of their former lord is extinguished; the other, that neither their laws nor their taxes are altered, so that in a very short time they will become entirely one body with the old principality.

When followers have much in common (language, culture, etc.), it is easier to keep their support. This is especially so when they have not been self-governed. When customs are alike, they can get along. Their leader must note two things: 1) The family of their predecessor has been killed, 2) They do not alter laws nor taxes. When these tenets are followed, in a short time, there will be unity in the nation.

But when states are acquired in a country differing in language, customs, or laws, there are difficulties, and good fortune and great energy are needed to hold them, and one of the greatest and most real helps would be that he who has acquired them should go and reside there. This would make his position more secure and durable, as it has made that of the Turk in Greece, who, notwithstanding all the other measures taken by him for holding that state, if he had not settled there, would not have been able to keep it. Because, if one is on the spot, disorders are seen as they spring up, and one can quickly remedy them; but if one is not at hand, they are heard of only when they are great, and then one can no longer remedy them. Besides this, the country is not pillaged by your officials; the subjects are satisfied by prompt recourse to the prince; thus, wishing to be good, they have more cause to love him, and wishing to be otherwise, to fear him. He who would attack that state from the outside must have the utmost caution; as long as the prince resides there it can only be wrested from him with the greatest difficulty.

When cultures within the community differ, the leader should live among them. Doing so, they can quickly respond to issues as they arise. Also, the country is not affected by unlawful officials when he is present. If not present, he would have to attack from the outside, which would be difficult.

The other and better course is to send colonies to one or two places, which may be as keys to that state, for it is necessary either to do this or else to keep there a great number of cavalry and infantry. A prince does not spend much on colonies, for with little or no expense he can send them out and keep them there, and he offends a minority only of the citizens from whom he takes lands and houses to give them to the new inhabitants; and those whom he offends, remaining poor and scattered, are never able to injure him; whilst the rest being uninjured are easily kept quiet, and at the same time are anxious not to err for fear it should happen to them as it has to those who have been despoiled. In conclusion, I say that these colonies are not costly, they are more faithful, they injure less, and the injured, as has been said, being poor and scattered, cannot hurt. Upon this, one has to remark that men ought either to be well treated or crushed, because they can avenge themselves of lighter injuries, of more serious ones they cannot; therefore the injury that is to be done to a man ought to be of such a kind that one does not stand in fear of revenge.

The leader would be wise to send colonies to various areas. Either this or have soldiers on the ready. It costs little and he ends up offending a few inhabitants in the colonies by taking their land/houses to give to the new inhabitants. Those who he offends end up scattered and powerless, so they cannot harm him. Those left behind keep quiet in fear for being put out of their houses. Inhabitants/men need to be treated well or totally crushed, because if crushed, they cannot heal and fight back. If injured enough, he would not fight back in fear of revenge.

But in maintaining armed men there in place of colonies one spends much more, having to consume on the garrison all the income from the state, so that the acquisition turns into a loss, and many more are exasperated, because the whole state is injured; through the shifting of the garrison up and down all become acquainted with hardship, and all become hostile, and they are enemies who, whilst beaten on their own ground, are yet able to do hurt. For every reason, therefore, such guards are as useless as a colony is useful.

Building an army in place of colonies is not effective. Soldiers become exhausted and bitter—turning against their leader. Colonies are useful.

Again, the prince who holds a country differing in the above respects ought to make himself the head and defender of his less powerful neighbours, and to weaken the more powerful amongst them, taking care that no foreigner as powerful as himself shall, by any accident, get a footing there; for it will always happen that such a one will be introduced by those who are discontented, either through excess of ambition or through fear, as one has seen already. The Romans were brought into Greece by the Aetolians; and in every other country where they obtained a footing they were brought in by the inhabitants. And the usual course of affairs is that, as soon as a powerful foreigner enters a country, all the subject states are drawn to him, moved by the hatred which they feel against the ruling power. So that in respect to those subject states he has not to take any trouble to gain them over to himself, for the whole of them quickly rally to the state which he has acquired there. He has only to take care that they do not get hold of too much power and too much authority, and then with his own forces, and with their goodwill, he can easily keep down the more powerful of them, so as to remain entirely master in the country. And he who does not properly manage this business will soon lose what he has acquired, and whilst he does hold it he will have endless difficulties and troubles.

The leader needs to make himself the head of, and defender of less powerful neighbors. He needs to ensure that no powerful foreigners gain power there. Existing inhabitants are drawn to the powerful foreigner because of the hatred they feel for their existing ruler. He needs to ensure that the nearby states that he does not rule remain in good will and less powerful than he. If he does not do so, he will have many troubles and may lose his acquisitions.

The Romans, in the countries which they annexed, observed closely these measures; they sent colonies and maintained friendly relations with* the minor powers, without increasing their strength; they kept down the greater, and did not allow any strong foreign powers to gain authority. Greece appears to me sufficient for an example. The Achaeans and Aetolians were kept friendly by them, the kingdom of Macedonia was humbled, Antiochus was driven out; yet the merits of the Achaeans and Aetolians never secured for them permission to increase their power, nor did the persuasions of Philip ever induce the Romans to be his friends without first humbling him, nor did the influence of Antiochus make them agree that he should retain any lordship over the country. Because the Romans did in these instances what all prudent princes ought to do, who have to regard not only present troubles, but also future ones, for which they must prepare with every energy, because, when foreseen, it is easy to remedy them; but if you wait until they approach, the medicine is no longer in time because the malady has become incurable; for it happens in this, as the physicians say it happens in hectic fever, that in the beginning of the malady it is easy to cure but difficult to detect, but in the course of time, not having been either detected or treated in the beginning, it becomes easy to detect but difficult to cure. This it happens in affairs of state, for when the evils that arise have been foreseen (which it is only given to a wise man to see), they can be quickly redressed, but

---

* See remark in the introduction on the word "intrattenere."

when, through not having been foreseen, they have been permitted to grow in a way that everyone can see them, there is no longer a remedy. Therefore, the Romans, foreseeing troubles, dealt with them at once, and, even to avoid a war, would not let them come to a head, for they knew that war is not to be avoided, but is only to be put off to the advantage of others; moreover they wished to fight with Philip and Antiochus in Greece so as not to have to do it in Italy; they could have avoided both, but this they did not wish; nor did that ever please them which is forever in the mouths of the wise ones of our time: Let us enjoy the benefits of the time—but rather the benefits of their own valor and prudence, for time drives everything before it, and is able to bring with it good as well as evil, and evil as well as good.

The Romans practiced this. It is important that a leader foresee potential issues, and addresses them before they become obvious. You have to have the right timing. Time can work in your favor if you are aware and proactive.

But let us turn to France and inquire whether she has done any of the things mentioned. I will speak of Louis* (and not of Charles)† as the one whose conduct is the better to be observed, he having held possession of Italy for the longest period; and you will see that he has done the opposite to those things which ought to be done to retain a state composed of divers elements.

---

* Louis XII, King of France, "The Father of the People," born 1462, died 1515.

† Charles VIII, King of France, born 1470, died 1498.

King Louis was brought into Italy by the ambition of the Venetians, who desired to obtain half the state of Lombardy by his intervention. I will not blame the course taken by the king, because, wishing to get a foothold in Italy, and having no friends there—seeing rather that every door was shut to him owing to the conduct of Charles—he was forced to accept those friendships which he could get, and he would have succeeded very quickly in his design if in other matters he had not made some mistakes. The king, however, having acquired Lombardy, regained at once the authority which Charles had lost: Genoa yielded; the Florentines became his friends; the Marquess of Mantua, the Duke of Ferrara, the Bentivogli, my lady of Forli, the Lords of Faenza, of Pesaro, of Rimini, of Camerino, of Piombino, the Lucchese, the Pisans, the Sienese—everybody made advances to him to become his friend. Then could the Venetians realize the rashness of the course taken by them, which, in order that they might secure two towns in Lombardy, had made the king master of two-thirds of Italy.

Louis of France did the exact opposite. It was not his fault, however, because he was forced to accept friendships with Italy, having no foothold there. All tried to befriend him.

Let anyone now consider with what little difficulty the king could have maintained his position in Italy had he observed the rules above laid down, and kept all his friends secure and protected; for although they were numerous they were both weak and timid, some afraid of the Church, some of the Venetians, and thus they would always have been forced to stand in with him, and by their means he could easily have made himself secure against those who remained powerful. But he was no sooner in Milan than he did the contrary by assisting Pope Alexander to occupy the Romagna. It never occurred to him that by this action he was weakening himself, depriving himself of friends and of those who had thrown themselves into his lap, whilst he aggrandized the Church by adding much temporal power to the spiritual, thus giving it greater authority. And having committed this prime error, he was obliged to follow it up, so much so that, to put an end to the ambition of Alexander, and to prevent his becoming the master of Tuscany, he was himself forced to come into Italy.

He could have been successful had he protected his weaker, more frightened friends. He weakened himself by helping Pope Alexander occupy Romagna. He alienated friends and aggrandized the church. Doing so forced him to Italy.

And as if it were not enough to have aggrandized the Church, and deprived himself of friends, he, wishing to have the kingdom of Naples, divides it with the King of Spain, and where he was the prime arbiter in Italy he takes an associate, so that the ambitious of that country and the malcontents of his own should have somewhere to shelter; and whereas he could have left in the kingdom his own pensioner as king, he drove him out, to put one there who was able to drive him, Louis, out in turn.

He also made an error by sharing Naples with the king of Spain. He was driven out.

The wish to acquire is in truth very natural and common, and men always do so when they can, and for this they will be praised not blamed; but when they cannot do so, yet wish to do so by any means, then there is folly and blame. Therefore, if France could have attacked Naples with her own forces she ought to have done so; if she could not, then she ought not to have divided it. And if the partition which she made with the Venetians in Lombardy was justified by the excuse that by it she got a foothold in Italy, this other partition merited blame, for it had not the excuse of that necessity.

It is natural to want more. If you succeed, you are praised, but if you do not, you are to blame. The acquisition of Naples was not necessary, and was, therefore, a greedy error.

Therefore Louis made these five errors: he destroyed the minor powers, he increased the strength of one of the greater powers in Italy, he brought in a foreign power, he did not settle in the country, and he did not send colonies. Which errors, had he lived, were not enough to injure him had he not made a sixth by taking away their dominions from the Venetians; because, had he not aggrandized the Church, nor brought Spain into Italy, it would have been very reasonable and necessary to humble them; but having first taken these steps, he ought never to have consented to their ruin, for they, being powerful, would always have kept off others from designs on Lombardy, to which the Venetians would never have consented except to become masters themselves there; also because the others would not wish to take Lombardy from France in order to give it to the Venetians, and to run counter to both they would not have had the courage.

Louis' Five Leadership Errors:
    He destroyed minor powers
    He increased the strength of greater powers in Italy
    He brought in foreign powers
    He did not settle in the country
    He did not send colonies.

He took the dominions away from the Venetians—he would have won them over had he not alienated then by aggrandized the church and brought Spanish into Italy. They were powerful and never would have been ruined, had he not done so.

And if anyone should say: "King Louis yielded the Romagna to Alexander and the kingdom to Spain to avoid war," I answer for the reasons given above that a blunder ought never to be perpetrated to avoid war, because it is not to be avoided, but is only deferred to your disadvantage. And if another should allege the pledge which the king had given to the Pope that he would assist him in the enterprise, in exchange for the dissolution of his marriage* and for the cap to Rouen,† to that

---

* Louis XII divorced his wife, Jeanne, daughter of Louis XI, and married in 1499 Anne of Brittany, widow of Charles VIII, in order to retain the Duchy of Brittany for the crown.

† The Archbishop of Rouen. He was Georges d'Amboise, created a cardinal by Alexander VI. Born 1460, died 1510.

I reply what I shall write later on concerning the faith of princes, and how it ought to be kept.

Louis did not avoid war, he deferred it. He erred on both accounts. As far as Louis supporting the Pope in exchange for the annulment of his marriage, I will speak of this later.

Thus King Louis lost Lombardy by not having followed any of the conditions observed by those who have taken possession of countries and wished to retain them. Nor is there any miracle in this, but much that is reasonable and quite natural. And on these matters I spoke at Nantes with Rouen, when Valentino, as Cesare Borgia, the son of Pope Alexander, was usually called, occupied the Romagna, and on Cardinal Rouen observing to me that the Italians did not understand war, I replied to him that the French did not understand statecraft, meaning that otherwise they would not have allowed the Church to reach such greatness. And in fact it has been seen that the greatness of the Church and of Spain in Italy has been caused by France, and her ruin may be attributed to them. From this a general rule is drawn which never or rarely fails: that he who is the cause of another becoming powerful is ruined; because that predominancy has been brought about either by astuteness or else by force, and both are distrusted by him who has been raised to power.

Louis did not follow the wisdom of those who had gone before him. The French did not understand strategy. If they did, they would not have let the church gain such power. In fact it has been said that the ruin of

France was due to their position with the church. There is a powerful saying, "He who makes another powerful is ruined." The reason being that the power came about through intelligence or force, neither of which is trusted by those who have become powerful.

STUDY GUIDE

Chapter III

Leadership Trait #3
Faith—Ability to Trust that Things Will Work Out

In this chapter, the author shares ideologies around how different beliefs, cultures and strategies affect one's area of influence. He encourages potential leaders to immerse themselves among those with whom they are seeking support and governance. In this segment you will explore faith versus force—how you believe you could best acquire leadership, and whether using force or true power would best serve you.

Faith—the ability to trust that things will work out is the leadership trait affiliated with this chapter. While believing that you are loved and guided in this world can be re-assuring, whether you are spiritually inclined or not, faith in yourself and in those who support you is essential to your success.

1. At the beginning of this chapter, Machiavelli asserts that difficulties often occur in new principalities or domains. People often change their leaders in hopes of finding someone better, but in the end, things are usually not improved upon. New leaders must thus burden those who support him or her with his soldiery. Thus by imposing force and might over the inhabitants, they try to instill trust. Write about a situation in your life or in the world at large in which someone has forced his or her power upon a new domain.

2. For the example in #1, did the individual or party achieve their desired results? Why or why not?

3. Some state that when you exert force to gain power, you never are truly powerful; that true power is earned based on respect. What are your views?

4. Authors like the late Dr. David Hawkins asserts that those who lead through force resonate at a lower level of consciousness, and therefore lack the energetic magnetism of one who leads through higher energy traits like integrity, honor, and authenticity. Share two examples of leaders, the first being someone who leads through force and the second being someone who has lead through example and positivity.

5. Look at the two leaders that you listed. Do you have any of the traits of the "forceful" leader? Do you have any that are reflected in the "honorable" leader? Do a comparison, and note which traits you have that you would like to change, and which you have that you embrace and appreciate.

6. Later in this chapter, the author makes reference to Louis XII, King of France. According to Machiavelli, he tried to take over leadership of Milan and lost because he treated the reigning prince poorly. What leadership initiatives do you have in your life?

7. Do your initiatives involve "overthrowing" someone else in power? If so, is there a way to do so that could create a win-win scenario? Explain.

8. Later in the chapter, Machiavelli shares that when followers have much in common (language, culture, etc.), it is easier to maintain their support. This is especially so when they have not been self-governed. What commonalities do the individuals you wish to lead share?

9. According to the author, when customs are alike, individuals can get along. If wishing to be effective, their leader must ensure two things: 1) The family of their predecessor (the previous leader) has been killed, 2) The new leader takes care not to alter laws, nor taxes. When these tenets are followed, in a short time, there will be unity in the nation. Of course, you would not take this suggestion literally, but how might you ensure that those you are working to lead are all on the same page? What action steps could you take to do so?

10. Another tenet that Machiavelli proposes is as follows: When cultures within the community differ, the leader should live within the community. Doing so, he or she can quickly respond to issues as they arise. There are two kinds of leaders: the individual who places himself on a pedestal, and the one who maintains relationships with his or her subordinates. While the separate leader appears to have more power, according to Machiavelli's theory, this is not so. In your own words, explain why.

11. The author later states that overthrowing leadership is much easier and more effective when the attack comes from within the city walls. Looking at an organization or area that you would like to lead, do you think you would have a better chance of acquiring leadership from within the infrastructure? Why or why not?

12. To paraphrase Machiavelli, he then suggests that the new leader would be wise to set up colonies to various areas. Either this or have soldiers on the ready. Doing so costs little and while he or she offends a few inhabitants in the colonies by taking their land/houses to give to the new inhabitants, they end up scattered and powerless. This initiative seems ruthless and harsh. Translating it to

present day leadership, what message do you think the author was sharing?

13. In such cases, those left behind will keep quiet in fear for being put out of their houses. He claims that people need to be treated well or totally crushed. If crushed, they cannot fight back. If injured enough, they would not fight back in fear of revenge. Are there other ways to lead beyond totally crushing your opponent? Cite examples of situations where you or someone you knew totally crushed the opponent to gain power. What was the outcome?

14. List at least one example of a situation where you or someone you know used a strategy other than brute force to gain power. What was the final outcome?

15. Which of these two methodologies was the most effective? Why?

16. Machiavelli further states that building an army in place of colonies is not effective. Soldiers become exhausted and bitter—turning against their leader. Do you think it best to fight your own battles or find support through others who assist you?

17. The leadership trait associated with this chapter is *faith— the ability to trust that things will work out*. Are there times when you lack the faith that others will support you? Write a list of those who provide you support.

18. Find at least three more supportive individuals to add to your support team. List them and write about why you would want them on your team.

19. Are you supportive of others? List ways in which you provide support to others.

20. Later in the chapter, the author states that the leader needs to ensure that the nearby states remain in good will and less powerful than he. If he does not do so, he will have many troubles and may lose his acquisitions. This reflects the well-known adage to keep your friends close and your enemies closer. What are your thoughts on this theory? Do you practice it? Why or why not?

21. Louis of France was forced to accept friendships with Italy, having no foothold there. He could have been successful had he protected his weaker, more frightened friends, but he weakened himself by helping Pope Alexander occupy Romagna. He alienated friends and aggrandized the church. Doing so forced him to Italy. Reflect on you previous leadership initiatives. Have you alienated others while asserting your power? If so, how?

22. According to Machiavelli, it is natural to want more. If you succeed, you are praised; however, if you do not, you are to blame. He asserted that the acquisition of Naples was not necessary, and was, therefore, a greedy error. Do an honest inventory with yourself. In the past, has your greed ever caused you to fail? For example, have you overspent money that you do not have? Have you pursued financial gain but in doing so, not acted in integrity? If so, write about your experience and any lessons you have learned from it.

23. The author outlines Louis' Five Leadership Errors as being:
    1) He destroyed minor powers;
    2) He increasing the strength of greater powers in Italy;
    3) He brought in foreign powers;
    4) He did not settle in the country he lead;
    5) He did not send colonies.

Reflect on a situation where you believed you have failed in your leadership initiative. List what errors you made. Then list what you did correctly.

24. Do you believe you have learned from the experience you described above? If so, how? If you believe you have never failed at a leadership initiative, how have you been able to maintain such success?

25. Machiavelli asserts that Louis did not follow the wisdom of those who had gone before him. Choose both a successful and an unsuccessful leader with whom you are familiar. What have you learned from each of them?

26. *Faithful—the ability to trust that things will work out* is the leadership trait affiliated with this chapter. On a scale from one to ten (one being "very little", and ten being "a great deal"), rate much faith you have that life tends to work itself out the way that it should:

1——2——3——4——5——6——7——8——9——10

27. List at least three examples of difficult situations where you noted that in the end, things worked out for the best.

28. On a scale from one to ten (one being "very little", and ten being "a great deal"), rate much faith you have in those that support your leadership initiatives:

1——2——3——4——5——6——7——8——9——10

29. Make is list of those who support you, and the ways in which you see them doing so.

30. Appreciation is a powerful tool. Successful leaders show appreciation and gratitude. Send a heartfelt note of appreciation to each of the individuals you listed in #32.

Chapter IV

Why the Kingdom of Darius, Conquered by Alexander, Did Not Rebel Against the Successors of Alexander at His Death

Considering the difficulties which men have had to hold to a newly acquired state, some might wonder how, seeing that Alexander the Great became the master of Asia in a few years, and died whilst it was scarcely settled (whence it might appear reasonable that the whole empire would have rebelled), nevertheless his successors maintained themselves, and had to meet no other difficulty than that which arose among themselves from their own ambitions.

After his death, Alexander's successors experienced no difficulty other than issues that arose among themselves.

I answer that the principalities of which one has record are found to be governed in two different ways; either by a prince, with a body of servants, who assist him to govern the kingdom as ministers by his favor and permission; or by a prince and barons, who hold that dignity by antiquity of blood and not by the grace of the prince. Such barons have states and their own subjects, who recognize them as lords and hold them in natural affection. Those states that are governed by a prince and his servants hold their prince in more consideration, because in all the country there is no one who is recognized as superior to him, and if they yield obedience to another they do it as to a minister and official, and they do not bear him any particular affection.

Principalities are governed in two ways: 1) Prince with servants (who are his ministers), 2) Prince with Barons who have bloodline—who have not been chosen by the Prince. In the second case, while no one is seen as more powerful than he, no affection is felt for the Prince.

The examples of these two governments in our time are the Turk and the King of France. The entire monarchy of the Turk is governed by one lord, the others are his servants; and, dividing his kingdom into sanjaks, he sends there different administrators, and shifts and changes them as he chooses. But the King of France is placed in the midst of an ancient body of lords, acknowledged by their own subjects, and beloved by them; they have their own prerogatives, nor can the king take these away except at his peril. Therefore, he who considers both of these states will recognize great difficulties in seizing the state of the Turk, but, once it is conquered, great ease in holding it. The causes of the difficulties in seizing the kingdom of the Turk are that the usurper cannot be called in by the princes of the kingdom, nor can he hope to be assisted in his designs by the revolt of those whom the lord has around him. This arises from the reasons given above; for his ministers, being all slaves and bondmen, can only be corrupted with great difficulty, and one can expect little advantage from them when they have been corrupted, as they cannot carry the people with them, for the reasons assigned. Hence, he who attacks the Turk must bear in mind that he will find him united, and he will have to rely more on his own strength than on the revolt of others; but, if once the Turk has been conquered, and routed in the field in such a way that he cannot replace his armies, there is nothing to fear but the family of this prince, and, this being exterminated, there remains no one to fear, the others having no credit with the people; and as the conqueror did not rely on them before his victory, so he ought not to fear them after it.

Two examples are Turk and the King of France. Turks are Lord and servants, and France, the King with ancient Barons. These Barons have their own initiatives that the King cannot counter. It would be difficult to seize the Turk state, however once done it would be easy to maintain. Harder to initiate, because it would be difficult to pull servants/ministers away from loyalty to the Prince. The revolter would have to rely more on his own strength than getting the Prince's ministers etc. to join him. Once the Prince is killed, there would be no fear of his staff turning against the revolter. He made his success because of his own strength without them, thus he need not fear them.

The contrary happens in kingdoms governed like that of France, because one can easily enter there by gaining over some baron of the kingdom, for one always finds malcontents and such as desire a change. Such men, for the reasons given, can open the way into the state and render the victory easy; but if you wish to hold it afterwards, you meet with infinite difficulties, both from those who have assisted you and from those you have crushed. Nor is it enough for you to have exterminated the family of the prince, because the lords that remain make themselves the heads of fresh movements against you, and as you are unable either to satisfy or exterminate them, that state is lost whenever time brings the opportunity.

With France it's easier because one can always enter through a discontented baron. Afterwards, however, it is not as easy to keep peace among those who assisted you and those you have crushed. Even if you have killed the Prince and his family, there will still be lords who will fight against you.

Now if you will consider what was the nature of the government of Darius, you will find it similar to the kingdom of the Turk, and therefore it was only necessary for Alexander, first to overthrow him in the field, and then to take the country from him. After which victory, Darius being killed, the state remained secure to Alexander, for the above reasons. And if his successors had been united they would have enjoyed it securely and at their ease, for there were no tumults raised in the kingdom except those they provoked themselves.

But it is impossible to hold with such tranquility states constituted like that of France. Hence arose those frequent rebellions against the Romans in Spain, France, and Greece, owing to the many principalities there were in these states, of which, as long as the memory of them endured, the Romans always held an insecure possession; but with the power and long continuance of the empire the memory of them passed away, and the Romans then became secure possessors.

And when fighting afterwards amongst themselves, each one was able to attach to himself his own parts of the country, according to the authority he had assumed there; and the family of the former lord being exterminated, none other than the Romans were acknowledged.

When these things are remembered no one will marvel at the ease with which Alexander held the Empire of Asia, or at the difficulties which others have had to keep an acquisition, such as Pyrrhus and many more; this is not occasioned by the little or abundance of ability in the conqueror, but by the want of uniformity in the subject state.

STUDY GUIDE

Chapter IV

Leadership Trait #4
Vulnerability—
Ability to Be Honest, Humble and Seen

Machiavelli opens this chapter by sharing information on how principalities are governed. Using the Turks and the King of France as examples, he then shares insights on the initiatives made by the leaders of the day. In the section, you will explore the three key steps to gaining support and loyalty. You will also investigate how you can strategically work with the existing powers in your organization in a way that best supports and serves your vision.

Vulnerability—the ability to be honest, humble and seen is the leadership trait associated with this chapter. Beware of leaders who lack these traits, for their emotional armor is too thick and they most likely lack self-awareness and healthy trust in themselves and others. There is a certain strength that comes with allowing oneself to be seen. When you cultivate a trust in yourself, and have a deep knowledge of who you are, you are more apt to allow yourself to be seen; to be vulnerable. Supporters become more trusting and are drawn to you when you are authentic, honest and humble.

1. Based on his experience, Machiavelli cites two ways in which Principalities are presided over, 1) By the prince

with servants (who are his ministers), or 2) By the prince with Barons who have bloodline (individual that he did not choose). In the second case, because their roles were inherited, they felt no affection or loyalty towards the Prince. It can be difficult to gain the respect and commitment of individuals who have more or less inherited their positions. As a new leader, list the benefits and challenges you would face in dealing with subordinates you had chosen. Then create the same list with those who have previously inherited their roles.

2. He cites two examples as being 1) the Turk and 2) the King of France. Turks are Lord and servants, and France, the King with ancient Barons. These Barons have their own initiatives that the King cannot counter. It would be difficult to seize the Turk state, however once done, it would be easy to maintain. This would be harder to initiate, because it would be difficult to pull servants/ministers away from loyalty to their former leader. The individual fighting for leadership would have to rely more on his own strength than getting the Prince's ministers etc. to join him. There are three key steps that a new leader could take to gain greater loyalty and support from their subordinates: 1) Display humility, 2) Lead with honesty and authenticity and 3) Credit any and all successes to the team.

3. On a scale from one to ten (one being "very little", and ten being "a great deal"), rate how much humility you have:

1——2——3——4——5——6——7——8——9——10

4. On a scale from one to ten (one being "very little", and ten being "a great deal"), rate how honest you are:

1——2——3——4——5——6——7——8——9——10

5. On a scale from one to ten (one being "very little", and ten being "a great deal"), rate how much you credit successes to others:

1———2———3———4———5———6———7———8———9———10

6. *Vulnerability—the ability to be honest, humble and seen* is the leadership trait associated with this chapter. If you are honest with yourself and others, then you also need to be willing to be vulnerable—open to admitting your errors, and owning your weaknesses. On a scale from one to ten (one being "very little", and ten being "a great deal"), rate how vulnerable you allow yourself to be:

1———2———3———4———5———6———7———8———9———10

7. Many have the mistaken belief that emotional vulnerability is a sign of weakness. Why would emotional vulnerability be powerful?

8. How have you seen emotional vulnerability benefit a leader and his/her subordinates?

9. In the case of France, the King entered through alignment with a discontented baron. In such cases, however, it is not as easy to keep peace among your subordinates and those you have overthrown. Even if you have killed the Prince and his family, there will still be lords who will fight against you. Taking this to your current leadership initiatives, list three additional strategies you can use to gain the support and loyalty of individuals who may not currently support you.

Chapter V

Concerning the Way to Govern Cities or Principalities Which Lived Under Their Own Laws Before They Were Annexed

Whenever those states which have been acquired as stated have been accustomed to live under their own laws and in freedom, there are three courses for those who wish to hold them: the first is to ruin them, the next is to reside there in person, the third is to permit them to live under their own laws, drawing a tribute, and establishing within it an oligarchy which will keep it friendly to you. Because such a government, being created by the prince, knows that it cannot stand without his friendship and interest, and does it utmost to support him; and therefore he who would keep a city accustomed to freedom will hold it more easily by the means of its own citizens than in any other way.

There are, for example, the Spartans and the Romans. The Spartans held Athens and Thebes, establishing there an oligarchy, nevertheless they lost them. The

Romans, in order to hold Capua, Carthage, and Numantia, dismantled them, and did not lose them. They wished to hold Greece as the Spartans held it, making it free and permitting its laws, and did not succeed. So to hold it they were compelled to dismantle many cities in the country, for in truth there is no safe way to retain them otherwise than by ruining them. And he who becomes master of a city accustomed to freedom and does not destroy it, may expect to be destroyed by it, for in rebellion it has always the watchword of liberty and its ancient privileges as a rallying point, which neither time nor benefits will ever cause it to forget. And whatever you may do or provide against, they never forget that name or their privileges unless they are disunited or dispersed, but at every chance they immediately rally to them, as Pisa after the hundred years she had been held in bondage by the Florentines.

But when cities or countries are accustomed to live under a prince, and his family is exterminated, they, being on the one hand accustomed to obey and on the other hand not having the old prince, cannot agree in making one from amongst themselves, and they do not know how to govern themselves. For this reason they are very slow to take up arms, and a prince can gain them to himself and secure them much more easily. But in republics there is more vitality, greater hatred, and more desire for vengeance, which will never permit them to allow the memory of their former liberty to rest; so that the safest way is to destroy them or to reside there.

STUDY GUIDE

Chapter V

Leadership Trait #5
Intuition—Ability to Trust the Voice From Within

Citing the Spartans and Romans as examples, in this chapter Machiavelli discusses the three means by which free states can be won: 1) Ruin them, 2) Reside within them, and 3) Allow residents to live by their own laws, maintaining an oligarchy that will keep it friendly to the new leader. He maintains that the leader who keeps his city accustomed to freedom, can hold onto it more easily. He continues by saying that a new leader who takes over a free city, and tries to maintain that state will surely be destroyed if he/she does not first destroy it. As with the case in Pisa, the inhabitants remember the name of their original leader of "freedom" and are not easily swayed by a new master.

The leadership trait affiliated with this chapter is *intuition—the ability to trust the voice from within.* While we are all born with an innate sense of knowing, many of our cultures do not support intuition, and insist on empirical evidence over inner knowing. Studies have shown, however, that the majority of Fortune 500 business leaders attribute trusting their gut instincts as a prime factor in their success. While you may not realize just how intuitive you are, as you focus your energy on developing trust in your inner knowing, it will subsequently become heightened. These skills will prove to be invaluable in your decision-making process as you pursue your leadership initiatives.

1. What does "freedom" mean to you?

2. What would "freedom" look like in your career life?

3. What would "freedom" look like in your personal life?

4. How would you define a "free state"?

5. According to Machiavelli, the three means by which free states can be won is to: 1) ruin them, 2) reside with them, and 3) allow residents to live by their own laws, maintaining oligarchy (a few number of residents ruling). Focusing on the area in which you would like to lead, do you believe that any of these three choices would work? Why or why not?

6. Have you ever experienced being led by someone who offered you a sense of freedom? How did it feel?

7. List both the benefits and drawbacks of having such freedom.

8. Have you ever had freedom that had then been taken away? What were the results?

9. To maintain order, especially in a free state, as a leader you have to have an inner and outer sense of trust. On a scale from one to ten (one being not very much, and ten being "a great deal"), rate how trustworthy you are of yourself and your own sensibilities.

1———2———3———4———5———6———7———8———9———10

10. An effective leader also must be able to delegate and trust her/his subordinates. On a scale from one to ten (one being "not very much", and ten being "a great deal"), rate how trustworthy you are of those who report to you (your subordinates).

1———2———3———4———5———6———7———8———9———10

11. *Intuition—the ability to trust the voice from within* is the leadership trait assigned to this chapter. What percentage of time would you say that you act upon your hunches, as opposed to logic?

12. The leadership trait affiliated with this chapter is *intuition— the ability to trust the voice from within*. Many of the world's successful business leaders trust their inner voice. In fact, many would argue that doing so is what makes them successful. Research your favorite business, political or social leaders, especially focusing on how much they trust their inner voice.

13. Have you ever had a hunch about something, and discovered that you were very accurate. Describe the situation.

14. According to the law of attraction, that which you focus your attention on grows. For the next month, focus on listening to your inner voice, and then acting on the hunches that it articulates. Keep a journal of your successful hunches, and then note if the number of hunches you receive grow. Most often they do because you are attentive to them.

15. Do you believe that trusting your inner voice would create a greater sense of freedom for you? How or how not?

16. List the ways in which you believe that trusting your inner voice could serve you as a leader.

17. Are there ways in which you believe that not listening to your inner voice can serve you as a leader? If so, how?

18. What three steps can you take to further develop and trust in your inner voice? List them and for the next month, take action on them. Journal about your experience.

Chapter VI

Concerning New Principalities Which Are Acquired by One's Own Arms and Ability

Let no one be surprised if, in speaking of entirely new principalities as I shall do, I adduce the highest examples both of prince and of state; because men, walking almost always in paths beaten by others, and following by imitation their deeds, are yet unable to keep entirely to the ways of others or attain to the power of those they imitate. A wise man ought always to follow the paths beaten by great men, and to imitate those who have been supreme, so that if his ability does not equal theirs, at least it will savor of it. Let him act like the clever archers who, designing to hit the mark which yet appears too far distant, and knowing the limits to which the strength of their bow attains, take aim much higher than the mark, not to reach by their strength or arrow to so great a height, but to be able with the aid of so high an aim to hit the mark they wish to reach.

I say, therefore, that in entirely new principalities, where there is a new prince, more or less difficulty is found in keeping them, accordingly as there is more or less ability in him who has acquired the state. Now, as the fact of becoming a prince from a private station presupposes either ability or fortune, it is clear that one or other of these things will mitigate in some degree many difficulties. Nevertheless, he who has relied least on fortune is established the strongest. Further, it facilitates matters when the prince, having no other state, is compelled to reside there in person.

But to come to those who, by their own ability and not through fortune, have risen to be princes, I say that Moses, Cyrus, Romulus, Theseus, and such like are the most excellent examples. And although one may not discuss Moses, he having been a mere executor of the will of God, yet he ought to be admired, if only for that favor which made him worthy to speak with God. But in considering Cyrus and others who have acquired or founded kingdoms, all will be found admirable; and if their particular deeds and conduct shall be considered, they will not be found inferior to those of Moses, although he had so great a preceptor. And in examining their actions and lives one cannot see that they owed anything to fortune beyond opportunity, which brought them the material to mould into the form which seemed best to them. Without that opportunity their powers of mind would have been extinguished, and without those powers the opportunity would have come in vain.

It was necessary, therefore, to Moses that he should find the people of Israel in Egypt enslaved and oppressed by the Egyptians, in order that they should be disposed to follow him so as to be delivered out of bondage. It was necessary that Romulus should not remain in Alba, and that he should be abandoned at his birth, in order that he should become King of Rome and founder of the fatherland. It was necessary that Cyrus should find the Persians discontented with the government of the Medes, and the Medes soft and effeminate through their long peace. Theseus could not have shown his ability had he not found the Athenians dispersed. These opportunities, therefore, made those men fortunate, and their high ability enabled them to recognize the opportunity whereby their country was ennobled and made famous.

Those who by valorous ways become princes, like these men, acquire a principality with difficulty, but they keep it with ease. The difficulties they have in acquiring it rise in part from the new rules and methods which they are forced to introduce to establish their government and its security. And it ought to be remembered that there is nothing more difficult to take in hand, more perilous to conduct, or more uncertain in its success, than to take the lead in the introduction of a new order of things, because the innovator has for enemies all those who have done well under the old conditions, and lukewarm defenders in those who may do well under the new. This coolness arises partly from fear of the opponents, who have the laws on their side, and partly from the incredulity of men, who do not readily believe in new things until they have had a long experience of them. Thus it happens that whenever those who are hostile have the opportunity to attack they do it like partisans, whilst the others defend lukewarmly, in such wise that the prince is endangered along with them.

It is necessary, therefore, if we desire to discuss this matter thoroughly, to inquire whether these innovators can rely on themselves or have to depend on others: that is to say, whether, to consummate their enterprise, have they to use prayers or can they use force? In the first instance they always succeed badly, and never compass anything; but when they can rely on themselves and use force, then they are rarely endangered. Hence it is that all armed prophets have conquered, and the unarmed ones have been destroyed. Besides the reasons mentioned, the nature of the people is variable, and whilst it is easy to persuade them, it is difficult to fix them in that persuasion. And thus it is necessary to take such measures that, when they believe no longer, it may be possible to make them believe by force.

If Moses, Cyrus, Theseus, and Romulus had been unarmed they could not have enforced their constitutions for long—as happened in our time to Fra Girolamo Savonarola, who was ruined with his new order of things immediately the multitude believed in him no longer, and he had no means of keeping steadfast those who believed or of making the unbelievers to believe. Therefore such as these have great difficulties in consummating their enterprise, for all their dangers are in the ascent, yet with ability they will overcome them; but when these are overcome, and those who envied them their success are exterminated, they will begin to be respected, and they will continue afterwards powerful, secure, honored, and happy.

To these great examples I wish to add a lesser one; still it bears some resemblance to them, and I wish it to suffice me for all of a like kind: it is Hiero the Syracusan.* This man rose from a private station to be Prince of Syracuse, nor did he, either, owe anything to fortune but opportunity; for the Syracusans, being oppressed, chose him for their captain, afterwards he was rewarded by being made their prince. He was of so great ability, even as a private citizen, that one who writes of him says he wanted nothing but a kingdom to be a king. This man abolished the old soldiery, organized the new, gave up old alliances, made new ones; and as he had his own soldiers and allies, on such foundations he was able to build any edifice: thus, whilst he had endured much trouble in acquiring, he had but little in keeping.

* Hiero II, born about 307 B.C., died 216 B.C.

STUDY GUIDE

Chapter VI

Leadership Trait #6
Focus—Ability to Stay With a Task

Machiavelli opens this chapter suggesting that those aspiring to greatness walk the paths that others have been beaten in, but imitate the ways to those powerful individuals before them when doing so. He references princes like Moses, Cyrus Romulus and Theseus in this chapter. He claims that they rose to power not because of good fortune, but because of their abilities. He also asserts that they maintained their power through force, using arms against any uprisings.

The leadership trait associated with this chapter is *focus—the ability to stay with a task*. In this fast-paced day and age, especially with the constant barrage of media interference through cell phones, computers and other technology, it can be particularly difficult to remain focused on the tasks at hand. Being organized and having the ability to quiet your mind of distractions can be key in further developing this trait in yourself. If you are not focused as a leader, the danger is that your lack of focus will infect your supporters as well. A focused leader maintains a focused group of staff and followers.

1. Machiavelli opens this chapter stating that *"A wise man ought always to follow the paths beaten by great men,*

and to imitate those who have been supreme." Are there individuals within your inner circle who you consider to be successful and wise men or women? If so, what strategies or behaviors do they practice that would also serve you on your leadership journey? If not, ideally you should surround yourself with those in the likeness that you aspire to become. How might you find mentors?

2. The author uses the analogy of the marksman who aims his or her arrow higher than the target, which is too difficult to hit dead on. By aiming high, the arrow has a better chance to hit its mark. How might this analogy apply to your leadership goals? What goals are currently too far out of reach, but are definitely a target you could hit?

3. The leadership trait associated with this chapter is *focus—the ability to stay with a task*. A good marksman is focused and steadfast. They stay with the task at hand, and practice their craft until they become proficient. On a scale from one to ten (one being "not at all" and ten being "a great deal"), rate how focused and steadfast you are when setting goals:

1——2——3——4——5——6——7——8——9——10

4. There are two different theories regarding focus and multi-tasking. While many claim that the ability to multi-task is a bonus, others claim that multi-tasking is not efficient and discourage it. What are your beliefs about multi-tasking?

5. Are you able to maintain focus on your leadership initiatives, or do you tend to get easily distracted? Rate your ability to focus from one to ten (one being "not at all" and ten being "a great deal"):

1——2——3——4——5——6——7——8——9——10

6. If you have not already done so, take some action steps towards finding a mentor whom you could emulate. Write about them, listing the traits that they have that you aspire to.

7. The author praises the leaders he lists in this chapter for taking the right action in response to the opportunities that came their way when he states, *"in examining their actions and lives one cannot see that they owed anything to fortune beyond opportunity, which brought them the material to mold into the form which seemed best to them."* Reflecting on your life, have there been opportunities that have come your way that you could have acted upon, but did not? List them.

8. Reflect on the list you created. What blocked you from taking advantage of those opportunities that came your way?

9. Imagine being given those opportunities now. How would you act in response to them?

10. Take at least three minutes and focus on visualizing the positive outcome that would come in response to acting upon these opportunities. Experience the success is as vivid a way as possible.

11. In each case Machiavelli shows how these leaders *"in their high ability"* recognized their opportunity, and in turn were made famous. Do an inventory of your life at the present time. Are there any current opportunities available to you? List them.

12. Write out an action plan for each opportunity you listed above. Then take that action. If you do not note any current opportunities, what steps can you take to create them?

13. In the examples in this chapter, Machiavelli maintains that the acquisition of power was difficult; however he goes on to say that they could not have maintained their power for long if unarmed. They often had to use force to persuade their people. Write at least one account where you have used force to gain power. What was the outcome?

14. After reflecting on the power that comes with knowledge, practice and focus, would you use force again if you had the chance? Why or why not?

Chapter VII

Concerning New Principalities Which Are Acquired Either by the Arms of Others or by Good Fortune

Those who solely by good fortune become princes from being private citizens have little trouble in rising, but much in keeping atop; they have not any difficulties on the way up, because they fly, but they have many when they reach the summit. Such are those to whom some state is given either for money or by the favor of him who bestows it; as happened to many in Greece, in the cities of Ionia and of the Hellespont, where princes were made by Darius, in order that they might hold the cities both for his security and his glory; as also were those emperors who, by the corruption of the soldiers, from being citizens came to empire. Such stand simply elevated upon the goodwill and the fortune of him who has elevated them—two most inconstant and unstable things. Neither have they the knowledge requisite for the position; because, unless they are men of great worth and ability, it is not reasonable to expect that they should know how to command, having always lived in a private condition;

besides, they cannot hold it because they have not forces which they can keep friendly and faithful.

States that rise unexpectedly, then, like all other things in nature which are born and grow rapidly, cannot leave their foundations and correspondencies* fixed in such a way that the first storm will not overthrow them; unless, as is said, those who unexpectedly become princes are men of so much ability that they know they have to be prepared at once to hold that which fortune has thrown into their laps, and that those foundations, which others have laid BEFORE they became princes, they must lay AFTERWARDS.

Concerning these two methods of rising to be a prince by ability or fortune, I wish to adduce two examples within our own recollection, and these are Francesco Sforza† and Cesare Borgia. Francesco, by proper means and with great ability, from being a private person rose to be Duke of Milan, and that which he had acquired with a thousand anxieties he kept with little trouble. On the other hand, Cesare Borgia, called by the people Duke Valentino, acquired his state during the ascendancy of his father, and on its decline he lost it, notwithstanding

---

* "Le radici e corrispondenze," their roots (i.e. foundations) and correspondencies or relations with other states—a common meaning of "correspondence" and "correspondency" in the sixteenth and seventeenth centuries.

† Francesco Sforza, born 1401, died 1466. He married Bianca Maria Visconti, a natural daughter of Filippo Visconti, the Duke of Milan, on whose death he procured his own elevation to the duchy. Machiavelli was the accredited agent of the Florentine Republic to Cesare Borgia (1478-1507) during the transactions which led up to the assassinations of the Orsini and Vitelli at Sinigalia, and along with his letters to his chiefs in Florence he has left an account, written ten years before "The Prince," of the proceedings of the duke in his "Descritione del modo tenuto dal duca Valentino nello ammazzare Vitellozzo Vitelli," etc., a translation of which is appended to the present work.

that he had taken every measure and done all that ought to be done by a wise and able man to fix firmly his roots in the states which the arms and fortunes of others had bestowed on him.

Because, as is stated above, he who has not first laid his foundations may be able with great ability to lay them afterwards, but they will be laid with trouble to the architect and danger to the building. If, therefore, all the steps taken by the duke be considered, it will be seen that he laid solid foundations for his future power, and I do not consider it superfluous to discuss them, because I do not know what better precepts to give a new prince than the example of his actions; and if his dispositions were of no avail, that was not his fault, but the extraordinary and extreme malignity of fortune.

Alexander the Sixth, in wishing to aggrandize the duke, his son, had many immediate and prospective difficulties. Firstly, he did not see his way to make him master of any state that was not a state of the Church; and if he was willing to rob the Church he knew that the Duke of Milan and the Venetians would not consent, because Faenza and Rimini were already under the protection of the Venetians. Besides this, he saw the arms of Italy, especially those by which he might have been assisted, in hands that would fear the aggrandizement of the Pope, namely, the Orsini and the Colonnesi and their following. It behooved him, therefore, to upset this state of affairs and embroil the powers, so as to make himself securely master of part of their states. This was easy for him to do, because he found the Venetians, moved by other reasons, inclined to bring back the French into Italy; he would not only not oppose this, but he would render it more easy by dissolving the former marriage of King Louis. Therefore the king came into Italy with the assistance of the Venetians and the consent of Alexander. He was no sooner in Milan than the Pope had soldiers from him for the attempt on the Romagna, which yielded to him on the reputation of the king. The duke, therefore, having acquired the Romagna and beaten the Colonnesi, while wishing to hold that and to advance further, was hindered by two things: the one, his forces did not appear loyal to him, the other, the goodwill of France: that is to say, he feared that the forces of the Orsini, which he was using, would not stand to him, that not only might they hinder him from winning more, but might themselves seize what he had won, and that the king might also do the same. Of the Orsini he had a warning when, after taking Faenza and attacking Bologna, he saw them go very unwillingly to that attack. And as to the king, he learned his mind when he himself, after taking the Duchy of Urbino, attacked Tuscany, and the king made him desist from that undertaking; hence the duke decided to depend no more upon the arms and the luck of others.

For the first thing he weakened the Orsini and Colonnesi parties in Rome, by gaining to himself all their adherents who were gentlemen, making them his gentlemen, giving them good pay, and, according to their rank, honoring them with office and command in such a way that in a few months all attachment to the factions was destroyed and turned entirely to the duke. After this he awaited an opportunity to crush the Orsini, having scattered the adherents of the Colonna house. This came to him soon and he used it well; for the Orsini, perceiving at length that the aggrandizement of the duke and the Church was ruin to them, called a meeting of the Magione in Perugia. From this sprung the rebellion at Urbino and the tumults in the Romagna, with endless dangers to the duke, all of which he overcame with the help of the French. Having restored his authority, not to leave it at risk by trusting either to the French or other outside forces, he had recourse to his wiles, and he knew so well how to conceal his mind that, by the mediation of Signor Pagolo—whom the duke did not fail to secure with all kinds of attention, giving him money, apparel, and horses—the Orsini were reconciled, so that their simplicity brought them into his power at Sinigalia.* Having exterminated the leaders, and turned their partisans into his friends, the duke laid sufficiently good foundations to his power, having all the Romagna and the Duchy of Urbino; and the people now beginning to appreciate their prosperity, he gained them all over to himself. And as this point is worthy of notice, and to be imitated by others, I am not willing to leave it out.

When the duke occupied the Romagna he found it under the rule of weak masters, who rather plundered their subjects than ruled them, and gave them more cause for disunion than for union, so that the country was full

---

* Sinigalia, 31st December 1502.

of robbery, quarrels, and every kind of violence; and so, wishing to bring back peace and obedience to authority, he considered it necessary to give it a good governor.

Thereupon he promoted Messer Ramiro d'Orco,* a swift and cruel man, to whom he gave the fullest power. This man in a short time restored peace and unity with the greatest success. Afterwards the duke considered that it was not advisable to confer such excessive authority, for he had no doubt but that he would become odious, so he set up a court of judgment in the country, under a most excellent president, wherein all cities had their advocates. And because he knew that the past severity had caused some hatred against himself, so, to clear himself in the minds of the people, and gain them entirely to himself, he desired to show that, if any cruelty had been practiced, it had not originated with him, but in the natural sternness of the minister. Under this pretense he took Ramiro, and one morning caused him to be executed and left on the piazza at Cesena with the block and a bloody knife at his side. The barbarity of this spectacle caused the people to be at once satisfied and dismayed.

But let us return whence we started. I say that the duke, finding himself now sufficiently powerful and partly secured from immediate dangers by having armed himself in his own way, and having in a great measure crushed those forces in his vicinity that could injure him if he wished to proceed with his conquest, had next to consider France, for he knew that the king, who too

---

* Ramiro d'Orco. Ramiro de Lorqua.

late was aware of his mistake, would not support him. And from this time he began to seek new alliances and to temporize with France in the expedition which she was making towards the kingdom of Naples against the Spaniards who were besieging Gaeta. It was his intention to secure himself against them, and this he would have quickly accomplished had Alexander lived.

Such was his line of action as to present affairs. But as to the future he had to fear, in the first place, that a new successor to the Church might not be friendly to him and might seek to take from him that which Alexander had given him, so he decided to act in four ways. Firstly, by exterminating the families of those lords whom he had despoiled, so as to take away that pretext from the Pope. Secondly, by winning to himself all the gentlemen of Rome, so as to be able to curb the Pope with their aid, as has been observed. Thirdly, by converting the college more to himself. Fourthly, by acquiring so much power before the Pope should die that he could by his own measures resist the first shock. Of these four things, at the death of Alexander, he had accomplished three. For he had killed as many of the dispossessed lords as he could lay hands on, and few had escaped; he had won over the Roman gentlemen, and he had the most numerous party in the college.

And as to any fresh acquisition, he intended to become master of Tuscany, for he already possessed Perugia and Piombino, and Pisa was under his protection. And as he had no longer to study France (for the French were already driven out of the kingdom of Naples by the

Spaniards, and in this way both were compelled to buy his goodwill), he pounced down upon Pisa. After this, Lucca and Siena yielded at once, partly through hatred and partly through fear of the Florentines; and the Florentines would have had no remedy had he continued to prosper, as he was prospering the year that Alexander died, for he had acquired so much power and reputation that he would have stood by himself, and no longer have depended on the luck and the forces of others, but solely on his own power and ability.

But Alexander died five years after he had first drawn the sword. He left the duke with the state of Romagna alone consolidated, with the rest in the air, between two most powerful hostile armies, and sick unto death. Yet there were in the duke such boldness and ability, and he knew so well how men are to be won or lost, and so firm were the foundations which in so short a time he had laid, that if he had not had those armies on his back, or if he had been in good health, he would have overcome all difficulties. And it is seen that his foundations were good, for the Romagna awaited him for more than a month. In Rome, although but half alive, he remained secure; and whilst the Baglioni, the Vitelli, and the Orsini might come to Rome, they could not effect anything against him. If he could not have made Pope him whom he wished, at least the one whom he did not wish would not have been elected. But if he had been in sound health at the death of Alexander,* everything would have been

---

* Alexander VI died of fever, 18th August 1503.

different to him. On the day that Julius the Second* was elected, he told me that he had thought of everything that might occur at the death of his father, and had provided a remedy for all, except that he had never anticipated that, when the death did happen, he himself would be on the point to die.

When all the actions of the duke are recalled, I do not know how to blame him, but rather it appears to be, as I have said, that I ought to offer him for imitation to all those who, by the fortune or the arms of others, are raised to government. Because he, having a lofty spirit and far-reaching aims, could not have regulated his conduct otherwise, and only the shortness of the life of Alexander and his own sickness frustrated his designs. Therefore, he who considers it necessary to secure himself in his new principality, to win friends, to overcome either by force or fraud, to make himself beloved and feared by the people, to be followed and revered by the soldiers, to exterminate those who have power or reason to hurt him, to change the old order of things for new, to be severe and gracious, magnanimous and liberal, to destroy a disloyal soldiery and to create new, to maintain friendship with kings and princes in such a way that they must help him with zeal and offend with caution, cannot find a more lively example than the actions of this man.

Only can he be blamed for the election of Julius the Second, in whom he made a bad choice, because, as is said, not being able to elect a Pope to his own mind, he

---

* Julius II was Giuliano della Rovere, Cardinal of San Pietro ad Vincula, born 1443, died 1513.

could have hindered any other from being elected Pope; and he ought never to have consented to the election of any cardinal whom he had injured or who had cause to fear him if they became pontiffs. For men injure either from fear or hatred. Those whom he had injured, amongst others, were San Pietro ad Vincula, Colonna, San Giorgio, and Ascanio.* The rest, in becoming Pope, had to fear him, Rouen and the Spaniards excepted; the latter from their relationship and obligations, the former from his influence, the kingdom of France having relations with him. Therefore, above everything, the duke ought to have created a Spaniard Pope, and, failing him, he ought to have consented to Rouen and not San Pietro ad Vincula. He who believes that new benefits will cause great personages to forget old injuries is deceived. Therefore, the duke erred in his choice, and it was the cause of his ultimate ruin.

* San Giorgio is Raffaello Riario. Ascanio is Ascanio Sforza.

Chapter VII

Leadership Trait #7
Oratory—Ability to Articulate Ideas and Initiatives

Machiavelli opens this chapter referencing individuals who rose to power solely due to good fortune. He later states that Duke Valentino laid solid foundations to support his future power. Seeking new alliances and temporizing with France, he showed boldness and ability. If Alexander had remained in good health, Machiavelli surmises that he would have overcome all difficulties. The duke was blamed for the election of Julius the Second, which, according to the author was his biggest mistake. At the end of this chapter, the author cautions, "he who believes that new benefits will cause great personages to forget old injuries is deceived."

The leadership trait affiliated with this chapter is *oratory— the ability to articulate ideas and initiatives.* One of the greatest downfalls of potential leaders is the lack of oratorical or public speaking skills. In order to gain a loyal army of followers, you must be able to communicate and connect with your audience in a passionate and heartfelt way. The good news is that there are many associations, tools and trainers who can assist you in becoming more confident and connected when speaking in public.

1. Machiavelli describes princes who were made by Darius in Greece as gaining power through "goodwill" and

"the fortune of him who has elevated him." He continues by stating these two opportunities as being "two most inconstant and unstable things." Reflecting on your life, when has what would be considered good fortune or luck played a part in your success?

2. Do you believe in being in the right place at the right time, or do you think that you had a hand in your "apparent" luck?

3. Were there any connections or occurrences that led up to your success that seemed like they were part of a pre-determined orchestration of synchronicities? If so, what were they?

4. Do you believe that the success would have occurred, even if you had not taken action steps towards your goal?

5. According to Machiavelli, Duke Valentino displayed bold-ness and ability in his ascent to leadership. Do you con-sider yourself to be bold? Explain.

6. An effective leader makes a heart connection with his or her followers, along with communicating a sense of hope and imminent victory. Without these three elements, loy-alty and trust can wane. After acquiring Romagna, part of the reason why the duke fell was that his forces "did not appear loyal to him." Most likely, he was not effective in communicating, incorporating the three elements. When you communicate to others, do you create a strong heart connection with them?

7. Are you positive, creating a sense of hope and imminent success when you lead?

8. What daily practices might you implement in order to instill connection, hope and a sense of victory with your subordinates?

9. Implement the regimen you listed in your response above, and note any changes that occur with your subordinates.

10. The duke secured himself in his principality by: winning friends, making himself beloved and feared by the people, gaining the loyalty and reverence of his soldiers, exterminating those with the power or reason to hurt him, changing the old order, maintaining friends with kings and princes. Reflecting on his actions, how might you secure greater power within your circle of influence?

11. The duke was blamed for the election of Julius the Second, which, according to the author was his biggest mistake. Have you ever supported someone into a position of power only to discover that doing so worked against your own power? If so, write about the event and what you learned from it.

12. At the end of this chapter, the author cautions, "he who believes that new benefits will cause great personages to forget old injuries is deceived." This statement asserts that old wounds are never forgotten. Do you believe this statement to be true?

13. What "old injuries" have you caused others that could impede upon your leadership ambitions? Write a list of individuals you have offended in your life.

14. List the ways in which you can make amends with each of the individuals you listed in your response to the previous question.

15. The leadership trait affiliated with this chapter is *oratory— the ability to articulate ideas and initiatives.* On a scale from one to ten, rate your overall ability as an orator (one being "not very effective" and ten being "highly skilled").

1——2——3——4——5——6——7——8——9——10

16. An essential aspect of being a great orator is having charisma. On a scale from one to ten, rate how much charisma you believe you have (one being "not very much"
and ten being "a great deal").

1——2——3——4——5——6——7——8——9——10

17. Another aspect of oratorical skills is the ability to organize
your thoughts in a way that is effectively communicated.
Are you good at organizing your thoughts prior to starting
a communiqué?

18. If you are not as organized as you would like to be, what
steps can you take to further improve upon your ability
to be more succinct and organized with your communi-
qués?

19. Another aspect of effective oratory is the ability to take
command over a room. There is an element of self-
confidence, and with that comes powerful projection—a
voice that can be heard. On a scale from one to ten, rate
how much well you project your voice (one being "not very
well" and ten being "very well").

1——2——3——4——5——6——7——8——9——10

20. Practice makes perfect when it comes to public speaking. There are public speaking coaches or organizations
like Toastmasters to assist you in improving your skills.
You can also practice your craft by joining leading local
sports teams, or volunteering in various associations or
onboards. List at least one step can you take to further
improve your oratorical skills.

Chapter VIII

Concerning Those Who Have Obtained a Principality by Wickedness

Although a prince may rise from a private station in two ways, neither of which can be entirely attributed to fortune or genius, yet it is manifest to me that I must not be silent on them, although one could be more copiously treated when I discuss republics. These methods are when, either by some wicked or nefarious ways, one ascends to the principality, or when by the favor of his fellow-citizens a private person becomes the prince of his country. And speaking of the first method, it will be illustrated by two examples—one ancient, the other modern— and without entering further into the subject, I consider these two examples will suffice those who may be compelled to follow them.

Agathocles, the Sicilian,* became King of Syracuse not only from a private but from a low and abject position. This man, the son of a potter, through all the changes in his fortunes always led an infamous life. Nevertheless, he

---

* Agathocles the Sicilian, born 361 B.C., died 289 B.C.

accompanied his infamies with so much ability of mind
and body that, having devoted himself to the military
profession, he rose through its ranks to be Praetor of
Syracuse. Being established in that position, and having
deliberately resolved to make himself prince and to seize
by violence, without obligation to others, that which had
been conceded to him by assent, he came to an understanding for this purpose with Amilcar, the Carthag-
inian, who, with his army, was fighting in Sicily. One
morning he assembled the people and the senate of Syracuse, as if he had to discuss with them things relating to
the Republic, and at a given signal the soldiers killed all
the senators and the richest of the people; these dead, he
seized and held the princedom of that city without any
civil commotion. And although he was twice routed by
the Carthaginians, and ultimately besieged, yet not only
was he able to defend his city, but leaving part of his men
for its defense, with the others he attacked Africa, and in
a short time raised the siege of Syracuse. The Carthaginians, reduced to extreme necessity, were compelled to
come to terms with Agathocles, and, leaving Sicily to
him, had to be content with the possession of Africa.

Therefore, he who considers the actions and the genius of this man will see nothing, or little, which can
be attributed to fortune, inasmuch as he attained pre-
eminence, as is shown above, not by the favor of any
one, but step by step in the military profession, which
steps were gained with a thousand troubles and per-
ils, and were afterwards boldly held by him with many
hazardous dangers. Yet it cannot be called talent to slay

fellow-citizens, to deceive friends, to be without faith, without mercy, without religion; such methods may gain empire, but not glory. Still, if the courage of Agathocles in entering into and extricating himself from dangers be considered, together with his greatness of mind in enduring and overcoming hardships, it cannot be seen why he should be esteemed less than the most notable captain. Nevertheless, his barbarous cruelty and inhumanity with infinite wickedness do not permit him to be celebrated among the most excellent men. What he achieved cannot be attributed either to fortune or genius.

In our times, during the rule of Alexander the Sixth, Oliverotto da Fermo, having been left an orphan many years before, was brought up by his maternal uncle, Giovanni Fogliani, and in the early days of his youth sent to fight under Pagolo Vitelli, that, being trained under his discipline, he might attain some high position in the military profession. After Pagolo died, he fought under his brother Vitellozzo, and in a very short time, being endowed with wit and a vigorous body and mind, he became the first man in his profession. But it appearing a paltry thing to serve under others, he resolved, with the aid of some citizens of Fermo, to whom the slavery of their country was dearer than its liberty, and with the help of the Vitelleschi, to seize Fermo. So he wrote to Giovanni Fogliani that, having been away from home for many years, he wished to visit him and his city, and in some measure to look upon his patrimony; and although he had not labored to acquire anything except honor, yet, in order that the citizens should see he had not spent his time in vain, he desired to come honorably, so would be accompanied by one hundred horsemen, his friends and retainers; and he entreated Giovanni to arrange that he should be received honorably by the Fermians, all of which would be not only to his honor, but also to that of Giovanni himself, who had brought him up.

Giovanni, therefore, did not fail in any attentions due to his nephew, and he caused him to be honorably received by the Fermians, and he lodged him in his own house, where, having passed some days, and having arranged what was necessary for his wicked designs, Oliverotto gave a solemn banquet to which he invited Giovanni Fogliani and the chiefs of Fermo. When the viands and all the other entertainments that are usual in such banquets were finished, Oliverotto artfully began certain grave discourses, speaking of the greatness of Pope Alexander and his son Cesare, and of their enterprises, to which discourse Giovanni and others answered; but he rose at once, saying that such matters ought to be discussed in a more private place, and he betook himself to a chamber, whither Giovanni and the rest of the citizens went in after him. No sooner were they seated than soldiers issued from secret places and slaughtered Giovanni and the rest. After these murders Oliverotto, mounted on horseback, rode up and down the town and besieged the chief magistrate in the palace, so that in fear the people were forced to obey him, and to form a government, of which he made himself the prince. He killed all the malcontents who were able to injure him, and strengthened himself with new civil and military ordinances, in such a way that, in the year during which he held the principality, not only was he secure in the city of Fermo, but he had become formidable to all his neighbours. And his destruction would have been as difficult as that of Agathocles if he had not allowed himself to be overreached by Cesare Borgia, who took him with the Orsini and Vitelli at Sinigalia, as was stated above. Thus one year after he had committed this parricide, he was strangled, together with Vitellozzo, whom he had made his leader in valor and wickedness.

Some may wonder how it can happen that Agathocles, and his like, after infinite treacheries and cruelties, should live for long secure in his country, and defend himself from external enemies, and never be conspired against by his own citizens; seeing that many others, by means of cruelty, have never been able even in peaceful times to hold the state, still less in the doubtful times of war. I believe that this follows from severities* being badly or properly used. Those may be called properly used, if of evil it is possible to speak well, that are applied at one blow and are necessary to one's security, and that are not persisted in afterwards unless they can be turned to the advantage of the subjects. The badly employed are those which, notwithstanding they may be few in the commencement, multiply with time rather than decrease. Those who practice the first system are able, by aid of God or man, to mitigate in some degree their rule,

---

* Mr. Burd suggests that this word probably comes near the modern equivalent of Machiavelli's thought when he speaks of "crudelta" than the more obvious "cruelties."

as Agathocles did. It is impossible for those who follow the other to maintain themselves.

Hence it is to be remarked that, in seizing a state, the usurper ought to examine closely into all those injuries which it is necessary for him to inflict, and to do them all at one stroke so as not to have to repeat them daily; and thus by not unsettling men he will be able to reassure them, and win them to himself by benefits. He who does otherwise, either from timidity or evil advice, is always compelled to keep the knife in his hand; neither can he rely on his subjects, nor can they attach themselves to him, owing to their continued and repeated wrongs. For injuries ought to be done all at one time, so that, being tasted less, they offend less; benefits ought to be given little by little, so that the flavor of them may last longer.

And above all things, a prince ought to live amongst his people in such a way that no unexpected circumstances, whether of good or evil, shall make him change; because if the necessity for this comes in troubled times, you are too late for harsh measures; and mild ones will not help you, for they will be considered as forced from you, and no one will be under any obligation to you for them.

STUDY GUIDE

Chapter VIII

Leadership Trait #8
Grounded—
Ability to Stand Rooted, Firm and Strong

Machiavelli opens this chapter citing two examples of how leaders rose to power through *"wicked or nefarious ways."* Agathocles, the King of Syracuse rose through the dedication and hard work through the army ranks. He ultimately assembled the people and Senate under the guise of speaking on behalf of the Republic, and ended up killing soldiers and those of wealth, overthrowing the princedom. His ability to deceive and slay could not be noted as "talent" that would align him with other great, respected leaders.

The second, Oliverotto da Fermo planned and executed the premeditated slaughter of his uncle, Giovanni Fogliani and his soldiers. Through this brutality, he secured the city of Fermo. The author concludes that if such injuries are done at all, then effective leaders should take the action and put away the sword. Otherwise, they will be forced to carry that sword throughout their leadership; security and ease would no longer exist.

The leadership trait that is linked to this chapter is being *grounded—having the ability to stand rooted, firm and strong*. If you look at a strong, large tree, you know that its roots grow deep into the ground. Like the tree, a grounded leader is level-headed, firm in his or her convictions, and shows strength. At the same time, however all trees sway in the breeze. An effective leader must also remain flexible in his or her ground-edness.

1. Agathocles' behavior appeared to be ruthless and merciless. Do you see yourself as exempt from such behavior? If so, reflect on a time in which you believed yourself to behave selfishly, where your desires took precedence over the welfare of others. Write about this experience. Did you learn anything from it?

2. Agathocles clearly manipulated his uncle. Are there times in your life where you realize you were manipulative? If so, describe them. If not, reflect on how you have been able to move beyond such behavior.

3. Have you ever been manipulated by someone and ultimately found yourself betrayed? If so, describe the experience. Did you learn anything from it? If so, what?

4. Is there ever a time when manipulation can be justified? If you believe there is, explain.

5. The leadership trait that is linked to this chapter is being *grounded—having the ability to stand rooted, firm and strong*. While the behaviors of many that Machiavelli discusses in this chapter are barbaric, in order to successfully carry out their plans, each of these leaders would have to be grounded. They would have to remain rooted, firm and strong. With the chaotic nature of life today, it can be especially difficult to remain grounded. On a scale from one to ten (one being "not at all" and ten being "very much"), rate how grounded you believe yourself to be (in general):

1——2——3——4——5——6——7——8——9——10

6. Many people fall short of their goals because they crash under pressure. On a scale from one to ten (one being "not at all" and ten being "very much"), rate how grounded you believe yourself to be when you are under pressure:

1——2——3——4——5——6——7——8——9——10

7. Do you have practices that you implement when you find yourself ungrounded? If so, what are they?

8. There are many techniques you can practice to ground yourself. One of those techniques is visualization. When you find yourself lacking focus, you can imagine yourself as the trunk of a strong tree, with roots growing deep into the center of the earth. Doing this exercise is a quick way to ground yourself, so that you are better able to focus. Next time you find yourself ungrounded, try this exercise and write about your experience before, during and after doing it.

9. Another grounding technique is to connect with nature. This can be as simple as taking a quick walk in a park, taking your shoes off and wading in sand, grass, or water. Practice this technique and note how you feel afterwards. Do you feel more focused and able to move forward in your work? Write about your findings.

Chapter IX

Concerning a Civil Principality

But coming to the other point—where a leading citizen becomes the prince of his country, not by wickedness or any intolerable violence, but by the favor of his fellow citizens—this may be called a civil principality: nor is genius or fortune altogether necessary to attain to it, but rather a happy shrewdness. I say then that such a principality is obtained either by the favor of the people or by the favor of the nobles. Because in all cities these two distinct parties are found, and from this it arises that the people do not wish to be ruled nor oppressed by the nobles, and the nobles wish to rule and oppress the people; and from these two opposite desires there arises in cities one of three results, either a principality, self-government, or anarchy.

A principality is created either by the people or by the nobles, accordingly as one or other of them has the opportunity; for the nobles, seeing they cannot withstand the people, begin to cry up the reputation of one of themselves, and they make him a prince, so that under his shadow they can give vent to their ambitions. The people, finding they cannot resist the nobles, also cry up the reputation of one of themselves, and make him a prince so as to be defended by his authority. He who obtains sovereignty by the assistance of the nobles maintains himself with more difficulty than he who comes to it by the aid of the people, because the former finds himself with many around him who consider themselves his equals, and because of this he can neither rule nor manage them to his liking. But he who reaches sovereignty by popular favor finds himself alone, and has none around him, or few, who are not prepared to obey him.

Besides this, one cannot by fair dealing, and without injury to others, satisfy the nobles, but you can satisfy the people, for their object is more righteous than that of the nobles, the latter wishing to oppress, while the former only desire not to be oppressed. It is to be added also that a prince can never secure himself against a hostile people, because of their being too many, whilst from the nobles he can secure himself, as they are few in number. The worst that a prince may expect from a hostile people is to be abandoned by them; but from hostile nobles he has not only to fear abandonment, but also that they will rise against him; for they, being in these affairs more far-seeing and astute, always come forward in time to save themselves, and to obtain favors from him whom they expect to prevail. Further, the prince is compelled to live always with the same people, but he can do well without the same nobles, being able to make and unmake them daily, and to give or take away authority when it pleases him.

Therefore, to make this point clearer, I say that the nobles ought to be looked at mainly in two ways: that is to say, they either shape their course in such a way as binds them entirely to your fortune, or they do not. Those who so bind themselves, and are not rapacious, ought to be honored and loved; those who do not bind themselves may be dealt with in two ways; they may fail to do this through pusillanimity and a natural want of courage, in which case you ought to make use of them, especially of those who are of good counsel; and thus, whilst in prosperity you honor them, in adversity you do not have to fear them. But when for their own ambitious ends they shun binding themselves, it is a token that they are giving more thought to themselves than to you, and a prince ought to guard against such, and to fear them as if they were open enemies, because in adversity they always help to ruin him.

Therefore, one who becomes a prince through the favor of the people ought to keep them friendly, and this he can easily do seeing they only ask not to be oppressed by him. But one who, in opposition to the people, becomes a prince by the favor of the nobles, ought, above everything, to seek to win the people over to himself, and this he may easily do if he takes them under his protection. Because men, when they receive good from him of whom they were expecting evil, are bound more closely to their benefactor; thus the people quickly become more devoted to him than if he had been raised to the principality by their favors; and the prince can win their affections in many ways, but as these vary according to the circumstances one cannot give fixed rules, so I omit them; but, I repeat, it is necessary for a prince to have the people friendly, otherwise he has no security in adversity.

Nabis,* Prince of the Spartans, sustained the attack of all Greece, and of a victorious Roman army, and against them he defended his country and his government; and for the overcoming of this peril it was only necessary for him to make himself secure against a few, but this would not have been sufficient had the people been hostile. And do not let anyone impugn this statement with the trite proverb that "He who builds on the people, builds on the mud," for this is true when a private citizen makes a foundation there, and persuades himself that the people will free him when he is oppressed by his enemies or by the magistrates; wherein he would find himself very often deceived, as happened to the Gracchi in Rome and to Messer Giorgio Scali† in Florence. But granted a prince who has established himself as above, who can command, and is a man of courage, undismayed in adversity, who does not fail in other qualifications, and who, by his resolution and energy, keeps the whole people encouraged—such a one will never find himself deceived in them, and it will be shown that he has laid his foundations well.

---

* Nabis, tyrant of Sparta, conquered by the Romans under Flamininus in 195 B.C.; killed 192 B.C.

† Messer Giorgio Scali. This event is to be found in Machiavelli's "Florentine History," Book III.

These principalities are liable to danger when they are passing from the civil to the absolute order of government, for such princes either rule personally or through magistrates. In the latter case their government is weaker and more insecure, because it rests entirely on the good-will of those citizens who are raised to the magistracy, and who, especially in troubled times, can destroy the government with great ease, either by intrigue or open defiance; and the prince has not the chance amid tumults to exercise absolute authority, because the citizens and subjects, accustomed to receive orders from magistrates, are not of a mind to obey him amid these confusions, and there will always be in doubtful times a scarcity of men whom he can trust. For such a prince cannot rely upon what he observes in quiet times, when citizens have need of the state, because then everyone agrees with him; they all promise, and when death is far distant they all wish to die for him; but in troubled times, when the state has need of its citizens, then he finds but few. And so much the more is this experiment dangerous, inasmuch as it can only be tried once. Therefore a wise prince ought to adopt such a course that his citizens will always in every sort and kind of circumstance have need of the state and of him, and then he will always find them faithful.

STUDY GUIDE

Chapter IX

Leadership Trait #9
Non-Reactivity—
Ability to take criticism impersonally

Machiavelli opens this chapter describing what he calls a "civil principality." In these cases, the leader comes to power not by violence, but by winning the favor of his fellow citizens. He states that a "happy shrewdness" is required in order to create this state. In such principalities, the new leader can rise from among the masses, or from nobility. Because the former arises from the general population, maintaining power is easier because he or she is seen as an equal. He goes on to share that it is easier to satisfy the people because their desire is not to be oppressed, whereas the desire of the nobility is to oppress. He also states that the leader can interchange the nobles who follow him; however he or she should not do so with the masses. Ideally the prince can win over the loyalty of the people by offering them protection, and by maintaining a friendly stance with them. He cites Nabis, the Prince of the Spartans as being a leader who was able to successfully do so. There is always a faithful following when a leader creates a sense of need in them and of the state.

Non-reactivity—the ability to take criticism impersonally is the leadership trait associated with this chapter. While some are naturally calm and non-reactive, most often non-reactivity comes with wisdom, insight and lots of practice. In order to be able to accept criticism, one has to be extremely confident. You have to be effective at knowing what your strengths and weaknesses are, and subsequently can see criticism as an opportunity for growth rather than a personal attack. Non-reactivity is a gift as anyone witnessing a non-reactive leader most often respects and admires their confidence and poise.

1. Knowing that a "happy shrewdness" is required in order to create and maintain a "civil principality," what leaders in the present or recent past exemplify a "happy shrewdness" in their leadership style?

2. Many effective leaders arise from the masses, and gain the respect and loyalty of their followers because of the adversities they overcame. Write about such leader, sharing details on what they overcame.

3. Often once one has been revered, they can easily fall from grace with an action that lacks integrity or is not honorable. Such was the case with Richard Nixon and the Watergate scandal. Write about such a leader and how they lost their post.

4. Have you ever made any dishonorable choices? What effect did it have on you and others?

5. Did you learn any lessons from your errors? If so, what were they?

6. Did you make amends with those you offended? If so, how?

7. Machiavelli asserts that leaders remain effective when they create a sense of need for them among their followers. Are you needed by those who follow you? If so, how?

8. If you do not believe that you are needed, how might you create a situation in which you may create a sense of need for your skills and services?

9. According to Machiavelli, effective leaders offer protection and maintain a friendly stance with their followers. How do you offer protection to your subordinates?

10. How might you offer more protection to your followers?

11. How might you extend a greater sense of friendliness to your followers?

12. The leadership trait listed in this chapter is *non-reactivity— the ability to take criticism impersonally.* On a scale from one to ten (one being "not at all" and ten being "a great deal"), rate much you personalize criticism:

1——2——3——4——5——6——7——8——9——10

13. One often gets defensive when they are very critical of themselves. Write a list of the traits that you criticize yourself for possessing.

14. Write a list of the traits you possess that you take pride in.

15. Review your two lists. Do you have more negative traits or positive traits listed?

16. Sometimes we does not focus enough on our accomplishments, thus are defensive and highly sensitive to criticism. What steps can you take to focus more on your victories and less on your challenges?

Chapter X

Concerning the Way in Which the Strength of All Principalities Ought To Be Measured

It is necessary to consider another point in examining the character of these principalities: that is, whether a prince has such power that, in case of need, he can support himself with his own resources, or whether he has always need of the assistance of others. And to make this quite clear I say that I consider those who are able to support themselves by their own resources who can, either by abundance of men or money, raise a sufficient army to join battle against any one who comes to attack them; and I consider those always to have need of others who cannot show themselves against the enemy in the field, but are forced to defend themselves by sheltering behind walls. The first case has been discussed, but we will speak of it again should it recur. In the second case one can say nothing except to encourage such princes to provision and fortify their towns, and not on any account to defend the country. And whoever shall fortify his town well, and shall have managed the other concerns of his subjects in the way stated above, and to be often repeated, will never be attacked without great caution, for men are always adverse to enterprises where difficulties can be seen, and it will be seen not to be an easy thing to attack one who has his town well fortified, and is not hated by his people.

The cities of Germany are absolutely free, they own but little country around them, and they yield obedience to the emperor when it suits them, nor do they fear this or any other power they may have near them, because they are fortified in such a way that everyone thinks the taking of them by assault would be tedious and difficult, seeing they have proper ditches and walls, they have sufficient artillery, and they always keep in public depots enough for one year's eating, drinking, and firing. And beyond this, to keep the people quiet and without loss to the state, they always have the means of giving work to the community in those labors that are the life and strength of the city, and on the pursuit of which the people are supported; they also hold military exercises in repute, and moreover have many ordinances to uphold them.

Therefore, a prince who has a strong city, and had not made himself odious, will not be attacked, or if anyone should attack he will only be driven off with disgrace; again, because that the affairs of this world are so changeable, it is almost impossible to keep an army a whole year in the field without being interfered with. And whoever should reply: If the people have property outside the city, and see it burnt, they will not remain patient, and the long siege and self-interest will make them forget their prince; to this I answer that a powerful and courageous prince will overcome all such difficulties by giving at one time hope to his subjects that the evil will not be for long, at another time fear of the cruelty of the enemy, then preserving himself adroitly from those subjects who seem to him to be too bold.

Further, the enemy would naturally on his arrival at once burn and ruin the country at the time when the spirits of the people are still hot and ready for the defense; and, therefore, so much the less ought the prince to hesitate; because after a time, when spirits have cooled, the damage is already done, the ills are incurred, and there is no longer any remedy; and therefore they are so much the more ready to unite with their prince, he appearing to be under obligations to them now that their houses have been burnt and their possessions ruined in his defense. For it is the nature of men to be bound by the benefits they confer as much as by those they receive. Therefore, if everything is well considered, it will not be difficult for a wise prince to keep the minds of his citizens steadfast from first to last, when he does not fail to support and defend them.

STUDY GUIDE

Chapter X

Leadership Trait #10
Objectivity—
Ability to See Reality Beyond Internal Struggles

This chapter opens with the examination of whether a leader is self-supportive, or requires the assistance of others. When requiring the aid of others, the leader needs to focus on fortifying his or her city, and avoid trying to expand their protection beyond the city and out into the country. Within the fortressed city, the leader should have sufficient artillery, food and drink for all inhabitants that would last at least one year. When the leader defends and supports his people, their loyalty grows and the city's strength against attacks is enhanced.

The leadership trait listed with this chapter is *objectivity—the ability to see reality beyond internal struggles.* Discerning fact from fiction and feelings from reality are a key element to becoming an effective leader. With many of the difficult decisions you make, it is imperative that you have the ability to determine truth from falsehood, leaving your personal feelings at the door. It also takes insight, honesty and introspection to be able to look at scenarios in a objective way, especially when things can appear to be very personally threatening.

1. It can take courage to request the assistance of others; however any wise leader welcomes help. He or she has the ability to recruit an excellent team and to delegate

responsibilities. On a scale from one to ten (one being "not at all" and ten being "a great deal"), rate how effective you are at seeking help from others:

2. Reflect on your life. List the times when could you have used more help with your initiatives, but avoided doing so.

3. Look at the list you created in the previous exercise. Write a list of the reasons why you hesitated to ask for help.

4. What steps can you take to overcome your discomfort with asking for help?

5. As previously mentioned, a great leader is able to delegate responsibilities. On a scale from one to ten (one being "not at all" and ten being "a great deal"), rate how effective you are at delegating responsibilities to others:

6. Often those who are unable to delegate fear that no one else could complete tasks as effectively as they can. They struggle to relinquish control. Do you believe this is sometimes the case with you?

7. Write a list of the traits that a subordinate would have to have, to ensure that you would feel comfortable delegating responsibilities to them.

8. Machiavelli asserts that a strong leader would have to be prepared by having enough food, ammunition, etc. for all inhabitants to last a year. Preparedness is an imperative for strong leadership. On a scale from one to ten (one being "not at all" and ten being "a great deal"), rate how effective you are in being prepared:

9. What three steps can you take to become even more prepared, so that you are confident and ready for any unforeseen challenges that may come your way?

10. The leadership trait for this chapter is *objectivity—the ability to see reality beyond internal struggles.* In order to be prepared and proactive, objectivity is important. By having an honest and nonreactive view of your situation, you are better able to handle it in an effective way. On a scale from one to ten (one being "not at all" and ten being "very much"), rate how objective you believe yourself to be, especially in heated situations:

1——2——3——4——5——6——7——8——9——10

11. In what kinds of circumstances do you note that you lose your objectivity?

12. Sometimes having an honest and loyal confidant who can gently call you on your reactivity can be helpful. Is there someone in your life who could fill that role for you?

13. Are there techniques or practices you can put into place that would help you to remain objective?

14. Part of being effective in your objective stance, is being able to see the big picture—how each of the components make the whole. On a scale from one to ten (one being "not at all" and ten being "very much"), rate how effective you are in being prepared:

1——2——3——4——5——6——7——8——9——10

15. In order to remain objective, it is necessary for you to believe in your inner sense of knowing. What steps have you taken to build your trust in yourself?

16. What step can you take to increase your faith in yourself?

17. When you are reactive, what do you do to move beyond your internal struggle and view the situation in an objective way? What do you further need to do?

Chapter XI

Concerning Ecclesiastical Principalities

It only remains now to speak of ecclesiastical principalities, touching which all difficulties are prior to getting possession, because they are acquired either by capacity or good fortune, and they can be held without either; for they are sustained by the ancient ordinances of religion, which are so all-powerful, and of such a character that the principalities may be held no matter how their princes behave and live. These princes alone have states and do not defend them; and they have subjects and do not rule them; and the states, although unguarded, are not taken from them, and the subjects, although not ruled, do not care, and they have neither the desire nor the ability to alienate themselves. Such principalities only are secure and happy. But being upheld by powers, to which the human mind cannot reach, I shall speak no more of them, because, being exalted and maintained by God, it would be the act of a presumptuous and rash man to discuss them.

Nevertheless, if any one should ask of me how comes it that the Church has attained such greatness in temporal power, seeing that from Alexander backwards the Italian potentates (not only those who have been called potentates, but every baron and lord, though the smallest) have valued the temporal power very slightly—yet now a king of France trembles before it, and it has been able to drive him from Italy, and to ruin the Venetians—although this may be very manifest, it does not appear to me superfluous to recall it in some measure to memory.

Before Charles, King of France passed into Italy,* this country was under the dominion of the Pope, the Venetians, the King of Naples, the Duke of Milan, and the Florentines. These potentates had two principal anxieties: the one, that no foreigner should enter Italy under arms; the other, that none of themselves should seize more territory. Those about whom there was the most anxiety were the Pope and the Venetians. To restrain the Venetians the union of all the others was necessary, as it was for the defense of Ferrara; and to keep down the Pope they made use of the barons of Rome, who, being divided into two factions, Orsini and Colonnesi, had always a pretext for disorder, and, standing with arms in their hands under the eyes of the Pontiff, kept the pontificate weak and powerless. And although there might arise sometimes a courageous Pope, such as Sixtus, yet neither fortune nor wisdom could rid him of these annoyances. And the short life of a Pope is also a cause of

---

* Charles VIII invaded Italy in 1494.

weakness; for in the ten years, which is the average life of a Pope, he can with difficulty lower one of the factions; and if, so to speak, one people should almost destroy the Colonnesi, another would arise hostile to the Orsini, who would support their opponents, and yet would not have time to ruin the Orsini. This was the reason why the temporal powers of the Pope were little esteemed in Italy.

Alexander the Sixth arose afterwards, who of all the pontiffs that have ever been showed how a Pope with both money and arms was able to prevail; and through the instrumentality of the Duke Valentino, and by reason of the entry of the French, he brought about all those things which I have discussed above in the actions of the duke. And although his intention was not to aggrandize the Church, but the duke, nevertheless, what he did contributed to the greatness of the Church, which, after his death and the ruin of the duke, became the heir to all his labors.

Pope Julius came afterwards and found the Church strong, possessing all the Romagna, the barons of Rome reduced to impotence, and, through the chastisements of Alexander, the factions wiped out; he also found the way open to accumulate money in a manner such as had never been practiced before Alexander's time. Such things Julius not only followed, but improved upon, and he intended to gain Bologna, to ruin the Venetians, and to drive the French out of Italy. All of these enterprises prospered with him, and so much the more to his credit, inasmuch as he did everything to strengthen the Church and not any private person. He kept also the Orsini and

Colonnesi factions within the bounds in which he found them; and although there was among them some mind to make disturbance, nevertheless he held two things firm: the one, the greatness of the Church, with which he terrified them; and the other, not allowing them to have their own cardinals, who caused the disorders among them. For whenever these factions have their cardinals they do not remain quiet for long, because cardinals foster the factions in Rome and out of it, and the barons are compelled to support them, and thus from the ambitions of prelates arise disorders and tumults among the barons. For these reasons his Holiness Pope Leo* found the pontificate most powerful, and it is to be hoped that, if others made it great in arms, he will make it still greater and more venerated by his goodness and infinite other virtues.

---

* Pope Leo X was the Cardinal de' Medici.

Chapter XI

Leadership Trait #11
Attentiveness—Ability to Actively Listen

Machiavelli opens this chapter by emphasizing the immense power that religious institutions had in the world of power and politics during his time. In such cases Princes have very little power, and those within their principalities are secure and happy. One of the challenges faced was the short life-span of most of the Popes (less than 10 years). He then goes on to review the performance of various powerful Popes in Europe's history. Pope Julius actually accumulated wealth for the church and in doing so, strengthened the power of the church. In the case of Orsini and Colonnesi, cardinals had been disallowed, thus protecting any rebels from building factions against the church and its power. Machiavelli ends this chapter exalting Pope Leo both for his power and his "goodness and infinite other virtues."

Attentiveness—the ability to actively listen is the leadership trait that is affiliated with this chapter. Active listening requires focus, confidence, commitment and selflessness. An active listener is not thinking about how he or she will respond to a speaker while they are talking, but are 100% attentive and present with the speaker. While it can take practice and a concerted effort, as you gain trust in your communication, strategic and leadership abilities, you will find that your charisma increases as you focus your complete attention on others, as opposed to yourself.

1. How do you believe religious institutions have gained such political power throughout the years?

2. What part does organized religion play in your life? Does it play any part or have an effect on your leadership goals?

3. What draws people to follow religious institutions?

4. Are you able to offer people anything similar? If so, what? If not, is there a way that you could offer them something similar?

5. In accumulating wealth for the church, Pope Julius became a successful leader. Do you currently have any wealth-building strategies in place? If so, what are they? If not, write a list of action steps you could take to further gain wealth.

6. Machiavelli praised Pope Leo for his "goodness and infinite other virtues." Write a list of the virtues you possess in which you are proud.

7. Among other things, an effect religious leader is often a successful listener. The leadership trait listed in this chapter is *attentiveness—the ability to actively listen.* On a scale from one to ten (one being "not at all" and ten being "very much so"), rate how effective you are as an active listener:

1——2——3——4——5——6——7——8——9——10

8. In order to actively listen, you need to be present with those who are speaking. To do so, you need to quiet your mind of its chatter. For the next week note how you respond when others are talking to you. Are you able to focus on them and quiet your mind?

9. You also need to have eye contact with the speaker and give them your undivided attention. Do you do so when others are speaking to you? For the next week, check in with yourself and note whether or not you do so.

10. Very often one focuses on what they will say next, and not on the speaker who is addressing them. Again, for the next week note your behavior when engaging with others. Are you thoughts on what you are going to say, or are you present with them? If you are thinking ahead into the conversation, try practicing being total present and attentive with the speaker.

11. One of the ways you can be more charismatic is to focus your attention upon others, as opposed to yourself. Practice focusing outside of yourself and onto being interested in others. In the beginning, you may have to fake it until you make it, but practice this technique, and make note of any changes you experience in doing so.

Chapter XII

How Many Kinds of Soldiery There Are, and Concerning Mercenaries

Having discoursed particularly on the characteristics of such principalities as in the beginning I proposed to discuss, and having considered in some degree the causes of their being good or bad, and having shown the methods by which many have sought to acquire them and to hold them, it now remains for me to discuss generally the means of offence and defense which belong to each of them.

We have seen above how necessary it is for a prince to have his foundations well laid, otherwise it follows of necessity he will go to ruin. The chief foundations of all states, new as well as old or composite, are good laws and good arms; and as there cannot be good laws where the state is not well armed, it follows that where they are well armed they have good laws. I shall leave the laws out of the discussion and shall speak of the arms.

I say, therefore, that the arms with which a prince defends his state are either his own, or they are mercenaries, auxiliaries, or mixed. Mercenaries and auxiliaries are useless and dangerous; and if one holds his state based on these arms, he will stand neither firm nor safe; for they are disunited, ambitious, and without discipline, unfaithful, valiant before friends, cowardly before enemies; they have neither the fear of God nor fidelity to men, and destruction is deferred only so long as the attack is; for in peace one is robbed by them, and in war by the enemy. The fact is, they have no other attraction or reason for keeping the field than a trifle of stipend, which is not sufficient to make them willing to die for you. They are ready enough to be your soldiers whilst you do not make war, but if war comes they take themselves off or run from the foe; which I should have little trouble to prove, for the ruin of Italy has been caused by nothing else than by resting all her hopes for many years on mercenaries, and although they formerly made some display and appeared valiant amongst themselves, yet when the foreigners came they showed what they were. Thus it was that Charles, King of France, was allowed to seize Italy with chalk in hand;* and he who told us that our sins were the cause of it told the truth, but they were not the sins he imagined, but those which I have related. And as they were the sins of princes, it is the princes who have also suffered the penalty.

---

* "With chalk in hand," "col gesso." This is one of the bons mots of Alexander VI, and refers to the ease with which Charles VIII seized Italy, implying that it was only necessary for him to send his quartermasters to chalk up th billets for his soldiers to conquer the country. Cf. "The History of Henry VII," by Lord Bacon: "King Charles had conquered the realm of Naples, and lost it again, in a kind of a felicity of a dream. He passed the whole length of Italy without resistance: so that it was true what Pope Alexander was wont to say: That the Frenchmen came into Italy with chalk in their hands, to mark up their lodgings, rather than with swords to fight."

I wish to demonstrate further the infelicity of these arms. The mercenary captains are either capable men or they are not; if they are, you cannot trust them, because they always aspire to their own greatness, either by oppressing you, who are their master, or others contrary to your intentions; but if the captain is not skillful, you are ruined in the usual way.

And if it be urged that whoever is armed will act in the same way, whether mercenary or not, I reply that when arms have to be resorted to, either by a prince or a republic, then the prince ought to go in person and perform the duty of a captain; the republic has to send its citizens, and when one is sent who does not turn out satisfactorily, it ought to recall him, and when one is worthy, to hold him by the laws so that he does not leave the command. And experience has shown princes and republics, single-handed, making the greatest progress, and mercenaries doing nothing except damage; and it is more difficult to bring a republic, armed with its own arms, under the sway of one of its citizens than it is to bring one armed with foreign arms. Rome and Sparta stood for many ages armed and free. The Switzers are completely armed and quite free.

Of ancient mercenaries, for example, there are the Carthaginians, who were oppressed by their mercenary soldiers after the first war with the Romans, although the Carthaginians had their own citizens for captains. After the death of Epaminondas, Philip of Macedon was made captain of their soldiers by the Thebans, and after victory he took away their liberty.

Duke Filippo being dead, the Milanese enlisted Francesco Sforza against the Venetians, and he, having overcome the enemy at Caravaggio,* allied himself with them to crush the Milanese, his masters. His father, Sforza, having been engaged by Queen Johanna† of Naples, left her unprotected, so that she was forced to throw herself into the arms of the King of Aragon, in order to save her kingdom. And if the Venetians and Florentines formerly extended their dominions by these arms, and yet their captains did not make themselves princes, but have defended them, I reply that the Florentines in this case have been favored by chance, for of the able captains, of whom they might have stood in fear, some have not conquered, some have been opposed, and others have turned their ambitions elsewhere. One who did not conquer was Giovanni Acuto,‡ and since he did not conquer his fidelity cannot be proved; but every one will acknowledge that, had he conquered, the Florentines would have stood at his discretion. Sforza had the Bracceschi always against him, so they watched each other. Francesco turned his ambition to Lombardy; Braccio against the Church and the kingdom of Naples. But let us come

---

* Battle of Caravaggio, 15th September 1448.

† Johanna II of Naples, the widow of Ladislao, King of Naples.

‡ Giovanni Acuto. An English knight whose name was Sir John Hawkwood. He fought in the English wars in France, and was knighted by Edward III; afterwards he collected a body of troops and went into Italy. These became the famous "White Company." He took part in many wars, and died in Florence in 1394. He was born about 1320 at Sible Hedingham, a village in Essex. He married Domnia, a daughter of Bernabo Visconti.

to that which happened a short while ago. The Florentines appointed as their captain Pagolo Vitelli, a most prudent man, who from a private position had risen to the greatest renown. If this man had taken Pisa, nobody can deny that it would have been proper for the Florentines to keep in with him, for if he became the soldier of their enemies they had no means of resisting, and if they held to him they must obey him. The Venetians, if their achievements are considered, will be seen to have acted safely and gloriously so long as they sent to war their own men, when with armed gentlemen and plebians they did valiantly. This was before they turned to enterprises on land, but when they began to fight on land they forsook this virtue and followed the custom of Italy. And in the beginning of their expansion on land, though not having much territory, and because of their great reputation, they had not much to fear from their captains; but when they expanded, as under Carmignuola,* they had a taste of this mistake; for, having found him a most valiant man (they beat the Duke of Milan under his leadership), and, on the other hand, knowing how lukewarm he was in the war, they feared they would no longer conquer under him, and for this reason they were not willing, nor were they able, to let him go; and so, not to lose again that which they had acquired, they were compelled, in order to secure themselves, to murder him. They had

---

* Carmignuola. Francesco Bussone, born at Carmagnola about 1390, executed at Venice, 5th May 1432.

afterwards for their captains Bartolomeo da Bergamo, Roberto da San Severino, the count of Pitigliano,* and the like, under whom they had to dread loss and not gain, as happened afterwards at Vaila,† where in one battle they lost that which in eight hundred years they had acquired with so much trouble. Because from such arms conquests come but slowly, long delayed and inconsiderable, but the losses sudden and portentous.

And as with these examples I have reached Italy, which has been ruled for many years by mercenaries, I wish to discuss them more seriously, in order that, having seen their rise and progress, one may be better prepared to counteract them. You must understand that the empire has recently come to be repudiated in Italy, that the Pope has acquired more temporal power, and that Italy has been divided up into more states, for the reason that many of the great cities took up arms against their nobles, who, formerly favored by the emperor, were oppressing them, whilst the Church was favoring them so as to gain authority in temporal power: in many others their citizens became princes. From this it came to pass that Italy fell partly into the hands of the Church and of republics, and, the Church consisting of priests and the republic of citizens unaccustomed to arms, both commenced to enlist foreigners.

---

* Bartolomeo Colleoni of Bergamo; died 1457. Roberto of San Severino; died fighting for Venice against Sigismund, Duke of Austria, in 1487. "Primo capitano in Italia."- Machiavelli. Count of Pitigliano; Niccolo Orsini, born 1442, died 1510.

† Battle of Vaila in 1509.

The first who gave renown to this soldiery was Alberigo da Conio,* the Romagnian. From the school of this man sprang, among others, Braccio and Sforza, who in their time were the arbiters of Italy. After these came all the other captains who till now have directed the arms of Italy; and the end of all their valor has been, that she has been overrun by Charles, robbed by Louis, ravaged by Ferdinand, and insulted by the Switzers. The principle that has guided them has been, first, to lower the credit of infantry so that they might increase their own. They did this because, subsisting on their pay and without territory, they were unable to support many soldiers, and a few infantry did not give them any authority; so they were led to employ cavalry, with a moderate force of which they were maintained and honored; and affairs were brought to such a pass that, in an army of twenty thousand soldiers, there were not to be found two thousand foot soldiers. They had, besides this, used every art to lessen fatigue and danger to themselves and their soldiers, not killing in the fray, but taking prisoners and liberating without ransom. They did not attack towns at night, nor did the garrisons of the towns attack encampments at night; they did not surround the camp either with stockade or ditch, nor did they campaign in the winter. All these things were permitted by their military rules, and devised by them to avoid, as I have said, both fatigue and dangers; thus they have brought Italy to slavery and contempt.

---

* Alberigo da Conio. Alberico da Barbiano, Count of Cunio in Romagna. He was the leader of the famous "Company of St George," composed entirely of Italian soldier. He died in 1409.

STUDY GUIDE

Chapter XII

Leadership Trait #12
Charisma—Ability to Draw People to Follow You

In this chapter Machiavelli starts his discussion on battle strategy and how to best defend one's state. He divides defensive structures into three states: The princes' own arms force, mercenaries, auxiliaries, or mixed. He believes that using mercenaries and auxiliaries is unadvisable and dangerous. He asserted that the ruin of Italy was easily procured by Charles, King of France due in large part to the utilization of mercenaries. He describes mercenaries as driven by greed and always aspiring to their own greatness, either by oppressing their leader or others. He then cited many cases in history where the mercenaries took away the freedom of the states they were hired to protect. In the end, he blamed the fall of Italy on the lowering of the infantry, having few foot soldiers, not killing their enemies, but taking prisoners and then liberating them without charging ransom. In their attempt to avoid fatigue and dangers, they made themselves vulnerable to the devices of Charles, Louis Ferdinand and the Switzers.

Charisma is the ability to draw people to follow you and it is the leadership trait outlined in this chapter. While it was mentioned in the last chapter that being an active listener enhances your charisma quotient, there are other practices and tools that can further assist you in becoming more charismatic. While many believe that charisma is a born trait (and often it is), you can develop greater charisma as you do your inner work. Gaining a deep faith and confidence in yourself, and looking beyond your personal goals towards supporting others is key to your success as a charismatic leader.

1. The means by which Machiavelli suggests protecting your state is not through the hiring of mercenaries and auxiliaries, but by your own leadership. Have you ever hired outsiders to support your leadership initiatives? If so, was the experience good or bad? Explain.

2. The author describes mercenaries as individuals who are *"driven by greed and always aspiring to their own greatness, either by oppressing their leader or others."* Write a list of individuals that you would describe as being selfish.

3. Write a list of individuals that you would describe as being greedy.

4. Were any of the individuals you listed in the past two responses leaders in their community or business? If so, would you consider them as being successful? Why or why not?

5. Do an honest appraisal of yourself. Are there times when you have been selfish? If so, are you critical of your self-ishness?

6. Do some further self-appraisal. Are there times when you have been greedy?

7. Often when we are critical of others, they have traits that we disown within ourselves. Do you criticize yourself harshly? If so, what can you do to be more patient and compassionate with yourself?

8. The leadership trait listed above is *charisma—the ability to draw people to follow you*. On a scale from one to ten (one being "not at all" and ten being "a great deal"), rate much charisma you believe you currently possess:

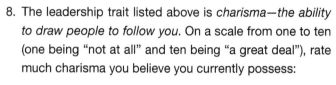

1——2——3——4——5——6——7——8——9——10

9. Do you believe that charisma is a trait that can be learned? If so, how?

10. Many charisma experts state that you become more attractive, the more you are interested in others (and not on yourself). On a scale from one to ten (one being "not at all" and ten being "a great deal"), rate how much you believe you are genuinely interested in others:

1——2——3——4——5——6——7——8——9——10

11. Could you cultivate greater interest in others? If so, how?

12. Do you think you can "fake" interest in others until you genuinely become more interested in them?

13. What action steps have you taken to enhance your charisma?

14. What further steps can you take to improve your charisma?

15. Think of the times that you have noted others were drawn to you. What were you doing? What was your frame of mind? Why do you think they became interested in you?

16. Often people are most attractive when they are "in the flow"—doing something they are very passionate about and enjoy. What are you most passionate about? Is there a way to integrate that into your leadership initiatives? Find ways to incorporate your "best" self into your public leadership initiatives.

Chapter XIII

Concerning Auxiliaries, Mixed Soldiery, and One's Own

Auxiliaries, which are the other useless arm, are employed when a prince is called in with his forces to aid and defend, as was done by Pope Julius in the most recent times; for he, having, in the enterprise against Ferrara, had poor proof of his mercenaries, turned to auxiliaries, and stipulated with Ferdinand, King of Spain,* for his assistance with men and arms. These arms may be useful and good in themselves, but for him who calls them in they are always disadvantageous; for losing, one is undone, and winning, one is their captive.

And although ancient histories may be full of examples, I do not wish to leave this recent one of Pope Julius the Second, the peril of which cannot fail to be perceived; for he, wishing to get Ferrara, threw himself entirely into the hands of the foreigner. But his good fortune brought about a third event, so that he did not reap the fruit of

---

* Ferdinand V (F. II of Aragon and Sicily, F. III of Naples), surnamed "The Catholic," born 1542, died 1516.

his rash choice; because, having his auxiliaries routed at Ravenna, and the Switzers having risen and driven out the conquerors (against all expectation, both his and others), it so came to pass that he did not become prisoner to his enemies, they having fled, nor to his auxiliaries, he having conquered by other arms than theirs.

The Florentines, being entirely without arms, sent ten thousand Frenchmen to take Pisa, whereby they ran more danger than at any other time of their troubles. The Emperor of Constantinople,* to oppose his neighbors, sent ten thousand Turks into Greece, who, on the war being finished, were not willing to quit; this was the beginning of the servitude of Greece to the infidels.

Therefore, let him who has no desire to conquer make use of these arms, for they are much more hazardous than mercenaries, because with them the ruin is ready made; they are all united, all yield obedience to others; but with mercenaries, when they have conquered, more time and better opportunities are needed to injure you; they are not all of one community, they are found and paid by you, and a third party, which you have made their head, is not able all at once to assume enough authority to injure you. In conclusion, in mercenaries dastardy is most dangerous; in auxiliaries, valor. The wise prince, therefore, has always avoided these arms and turned to his own; and has been willing rather to lose with them than to conquer with the others, not deeming that a real victory which is gained with the arms of others.

---

* Joannes Cantacuzenus, born 1300, died 1383.

I shall never hesitate to cite Cesare Borgia and his actions. This duke entered the Romagna with auxiliaries, taking there only French soldiers, and with them he captured Imola and Forli; but afterwards, such forces not appearing to him reliable, he turned to mercenaries, discerning less danger in them, and enlisted the Orsini and Vitelli; whom presently, on handling and finding them doubtful, unfaithful, and dangerous, he destroyed and turned to his own men. And the difference between one and the other of these forces can easily be seen when one considers the difference there was in the reputation of the duke, when he had the French, when he had the Orsini and Vitelli, and when he relied on his own soldiers, on whose fidelity he could always count and found it ever increasing; he was never esteemed more highly than when everyone saw that he was complete master of his own forces.

I was not intending to go beyond Italian and recent examples, but I am unwilling to leave out Hiero, the Syracusan, he being one of those I have named above. This man, as I have said, made head of the army by the Syracusans, soon found out that a mercenary soldiery, constituted like our Italian condottieri, was of no use; and it appearing to him that he could neither keep them not let them go, he had them all cut to pieces, and afterwards made war with his own forces and not with aliens.

I wish also to recall to memory an instance from the Old Testament applicable to this subject. David offered himself to Saul to fight with Goliath, the Philistine

champion, and, to give him courage; Saul armed him
with his own weapons; which David rejected as soon as
he had them on his back, saying he could make no use
of them, and that he wished to meet the enemy with his
sling and his knife. In conclusion, the arms of others either fall from your back, or they weigh you down, or they
bind you fast.

Charles the Seventh,* the father of King Louis† the
Eleventh, having by good fortune and valor liberated
France from the English, recognized the necessity of
being armed with forces of his own, and he established
in his kingdom ordinances concerning men-at-arms and
infantry. Afterwards his son, King Louis, abolished the
infantry and began to enlist the Switzers, which mistake, followed by others, is, as is now seen, a source of
peril to that kingdom; because, having raised the reputation of the Switzers, he has entirely diminished the
value of his own arms, for he has destroyed the infantry
altogether; and his men-at-arms he has subordinated to
others, for, being as they are so accustomed to fight along
with Switzers, it does not appear that they can now conquer without them. Hence it arises that the French cannot stand against the Switzers, and without the Switzers
they do not come off well against others. The armies of
the French have thus become mixed, partly mercenary
and partly national, both of which arms together are
much better than mercenaries alone or auxiliaries alone,

---

* Charles VII of France, surnamed "The Victorious," born 1403, died 1461.

† Louis XI, son of the above, born 1423, died 1483.

but much inferior to one's own forces. And this example proves it, for the kingdom of France would be unconquerable if the ordinance of Charles had been enlarged or maintained.

But the scanty wisdom of man, on entering into an affair which looks well at first, cannot discern the poison that is hidden in it, as I have said above of hectic fevers. Therefore, if he who rules a principality cannot recognize evils until they are upon him, he is not truly wise; and this insight is given to few. And if the first disaster to the Roman Empire* should be examined, it will be found to have commenced only with the enlisting of the Goths; because from that time the vigor of the Roman Empire began to decline, and all that valor which had raised it passed away to others.

I conclude, therefore, that no principality is secure without having its own forces; on the contrary, it is entirely dependent on good fortune, not having the valor which in adversity would defend it. And it has always been the opinion and judgment of wise men that nothing can be so uncertain or unstable as fame or power not founded on its own strength. And one's own forces are those which are composed either of subjects, citizens, or dependents; all others are mercenaries or auxiliaries.

---

* "Many speakers to the House the other night in the debate on the reduction of armaments seemed to show a most lamentable ignorance of the conditions under which the British Empire maintains its existence. When Mr. Balfour replied to the allegations that the Roman Empire sank under the weight of its military obligations, he said that this was 'wholly unhistorical.' He might well have added that the Roman power was at its zenith when every citizen acknowledged his liability to fight for the State, but that it began to decline as soon as this obligation was no longer recognized."—Pall Mall Gazette, 15th May 1906.

And the way to make ready one's own forces will be easily found if the rules suggested by me shall be reflected upon, and if one will consider how Philip, the father of Alexander the Great, and many republics and princes have armed and organized themselves, to which rules I entirely commit myself.

Chapter XIII

Leadership Trait #13
Recruitment—
Ability to See and Seek Talent in Others

In the chapter, Machiavelli shares his observations and insights on the employment of auxiliaries. He references several examples of the unsuccessful use of auxiliaries during his time, stating that using them is even worse that using mercenaries because they are united and ruin is ready-made. He then cites Cesare Borgia and an account of what transpired when he and his auxiliaries entered Romagna. He concluded that Borgia was never more esteemed than when he fought with his own forces. He then shared the story of David's slaying of Goliath in the Old Testament as an example of how effective David was when he rejected Saul's weapons and used his own. Another example he shares is of Charles the Seventh and his son, King Louis. Armed with his own forces, Charles was a great success and established a victorious kingdom until his son King Louis abolished the infantry and enlisted the Switzers. He later states that those who cannot recognize evils when they are upon him, lacks wisdom—as was the case with the Roman Empire when they enlisted the Goths. He concludes that no principality is secure without using its own forces, and cites how Philip, the father of Alexander the Great and others armed and organized themselves. They did so in a way that Machiavelli respected and revered.

The ability to see and seek talent in others, to be an excellent recruiter is the leadership trait affiliated with this chapter. An effective leader is only as strong as his or her team is. The ability to read people and determine if and how they could best work for your organization is a gift that all leaders would do well to integrate into their leadership initiatives. While the ability to read others often involves an innate sense, there are practices and tools to help you develop this skill.

1. At first glance, one might anticipate that joining forces with a neighboring army could strengthen one's strategic position, however in this chapter, Machiavelli discourages it. Make a list of how enlisting the aid of others might support you in your leadership initiatives.

2. Make a list of how getting assistance from others may, in fact weaken you as a leader.

3. How might the strong unification of a group or community you enlist negatively affect your leadership efforts?

4. Have you even been responsible for assembling a strong group of supporters? If so, how did you enlist them? What techniques did you use to gain their loyalty and trust?

5. David had few weapons, yet he successfully beat Goliath. Why do you think he was able to do so?

6. Do you think that David had faith in a benevolent, supportive God? If so, was that faith central to his victory?

7. Machiavelli claims that those who do not recognize evil lack wisdom. On a scale from one to ten (one being "not at all" and ten being "a great deal"), rate much faith you have that you will be protected and supported in your future leadership endeavors:

1——2——3——4——5——6——7——8——9——10

8. Do you believe that you can you strengthen your faith? If so, how? If not, why not?

9. The leadership trait referenced in this chapter is *recruitment—the ability to see and seek talent in others.* How important do you believe this skill is for leaders to be effective?

10. In order to be an effective recruiter, one needs to be able to know where to find talented followers. On a scale from one to ten (one being "not at all" and ten being "very much so"), rate how effective you are at recruiting effective subordinates:

1——2——3——4——5——6——7——8——9——10

11. A successful recruiter also needs to be able to effectively communicate what is expected of the follower, and to have the ability to articulate their needs. On a scale from one to ten (one being "not at all" and ten being "very much so"), rate how effective you are at communicating your needs:

1——2——3——4——5——6——7——8——9——10

12. It is also important that you, as a recruiter position the opportunity in a way that creates great enthusiasm in the potential colleague. On a scale from one to ten (one being "not at all" and ten being "very much so"), rate how effective you are at sparking enthusiasm in potential recruits:

1——2——3——4——5——6——7——8——9——10

13. What steps can you take in your recruitment initiatives to create more enthusiasm among perspective recruits?

14. What recruitment tools and techniques do you currently use (newspaper, internet, agencies, etc.)?

15. Do you ever recruit through local one-on-one connections? Explain.

16. On a scale from one to ten (one being "not at all" and ten being "very much so"), rate how effective you are at reading people, getting a sense who they are, quickly and intuitively:

1——2——3——4——5——6——7——8——9——10

17. How might you further develop your intuitive skills when it comes to getting a sense of how others tick?

18. Are you effective at clarifying and articulating with others what your needs are and how they can assist you in fulfilling them?

19. How might you improve your communication skills (oral and written)?

20. Write out a strategy that will assist you in further recruiting followers. Be sure to be specific on dates, times, methodology and success tracking when doing so.

Chapter XIV

That Which Concerns A Prince on the Subject of the Art of War

A prince ought to have no other aim or thought, nor select anything else for his study, than war and its rules and discipline; for this is the sole art that belongs to him who rules, and it is of such force that it not only upholds those who are born princes, but it often enables men to rise from a private station to that rank. And, on the contrary, it is seen that when princes have thought more of ease than of arms they have lost their states. And the first cause of your losing it is to neglect this art; and what enables you to acquire a state is to be master of the art. Francesco Sforza, through being martial, from a private person became Duke of Milan; and the sons, through avoiding the hardships and troubles of arms, from dukes became private persons. For among other evils which being unarmed brings you, it causes you to be despised, and this is one of those ignominies against which a prince ought to guard himself, as is shown later on. Because there is nothing proportionate between the armed and the unarmed; and it is not reasonable that he who is armed should yield obedience willingly to him who is unarmed, or that the unarmed man should be secure among armed servants. Because, there being in the one disdain and in the other suspicion, it is not possible for them to work well together. And therefore a prince who does not understand the art of war, over and above the other misfortunes already mentioned, cannot be respected by his soldiers, nor can he rely on them. He ought never, therefore, to have out of his thoughts this subject of war, and in peace he should addict himself more to its exercise than in war; this he can do in two ways, the one by action, the other by study.

As regards action, he ought above all things to keep his men well organized and drilled, to follow incessantly the chase, by which he accustoms his body to hardships, and learns something of the nature of localities, and gets to find out how the mountains rise, how the valleys open out, how the plains lie, and to understand the nature of rivers and marshes, and in all this to take the greatest care. Which knowledge is useful in two ways. Firstly, he learns to know his country, and is better able to undertake its defense; afterwards, by means of the knowledge and observation of that locality, he understands with ease any other which it may be necessary for him to study hereafter; because the hills, valleys, and plains, and rivers and marshes that are, for instance, in Tuscany, have a certain resemblance to those of other countries, so that with a knowledge of the aspect of one country one can easily arrive at a knowledge of others. And the prince that lacks this skill lacks the essential which it is desirable that a captain should possess, for it teaches him to surprise his enemy, to select quarters, to lead armies, to array the battle, to besiege towns to advantage.

Philopoemen,* Prince of the Achaeans, among other praises which writers have bestowed on him, is commended because in time of peace he never had anything in his mind but the rules of war; and when he was in the country with friends, he often stopped and reasoned with them: "If the enemy should be upon that hill, and we should find ourselves here with our army, with whom would be the advantage? How should one best advance to meet him, keeping the ranks? If we should wish to retreat, how ought we to pursue?" And he would set forth to them, as he went, all the chances that could befall an army; he would listen to their opinion and state his, confirming it with reasons, so that by these continual discussions there could never arise, in time of war, any unexpected circumstances that he could not deal with.

But to exercise the intellect the prince should read histories, and study there the actions of illustrious men, to see how they have borne themselves in war, to examine the causes of their victories and defeat, so as to avoid the latter and imitate the former; and above all do as an illustrious man did, who took as an exemplar one who had been praised and famous before him, and whose achievements and deeds he always kept in his mind, as it is said Alexander the Great imitated Achilles, Caesar Alexander, Scipio Cyrus. And whoever reads the life of

---

* Philopoemen, "the last of the Greeks," born 252 B.C., died 183 B.C.

Cyrus, written by Xenophon, will recognize afterwards in the life of Scipio how that imitation was his glory, and how in chastity, affability, humanity, and liberality Scipio conformed to those things which have been written of Cyrus by Xenophon. A wise prince ought to observe some such rules, and never in peaceful times stand idle, but increase his resources with industry in such a way that they may be available to him in adversity, so that if fortune chances it may find him prepared to resist her blows.

Chapter XIV

Leadership Trait #14
Strength—
Ability to Maintain Physical and Emotional Strength

Machiavelli opens this chapter, emphasizing that a prince (or leader) should be intimately familiar with the rules and disciplines of war. He claims that *"princes who thought more of ease than arms they have lost their states."* He cites the example of Francesco Sforza and his rise to the position of Duke of Milan as being a prime example of this. He claims that distain and suspicion exist between the armed and the unarmed, and asserts that leaders who do not understand the art of war, will not be respected by their soldiers, nor can they rely upon them. Leaders need to understand war by mastering two practices: action and study. In regards to action, he or she needs to 1) keep his men well organized, 2) drill his men on a regular basis, 3) accustom his body to hardships and 4) understand the terrain that he/she is entering. Machiavelli then commended Philopoemen, the Prince of the Achaeans for always studying his surroundings and discussing potential war strategies with others, even during peaceful times, so that he would always be best strategically prepared should warfare arise. The author also stipulates that in order to "exercise the intellect" the prince should 1) read histories, 2) study the actions of illustrious men and 3) follow the actions of wise and successful leaders before him. He ended this chapter with the assertion that a wise prince never stands idle, whether in peaceful times or in warfare.

The ability to maintain physical and emotional strength is the leadership trait associated with this chapter. It is important that leaders maintain strength, not only physically, but mentally and emotionally as well. When you are healthy, steadfast and strong in all areas of your life, you are better able to face whatever challenges come your way. Strength does not always show up in brute force. Often strength is the ability to be subtle and graceful in your interactions.

1. While you may not be at "war" in your leadership initiatives, the guidelines that Machiavelli outlines in this chapter would still apply. Are you familiar with the rules and disciplines that surround the subject matter that you are pursuing?

2. The author also encourages you remaining alert and researching strategies and the playing field within which you are active. On a scale from one to ten (one being "not at all" and ten being "a great deal"), rate how actively you research your playing field on an ongoing basis:

1———2———3———4———5———6———7———8———9———10

3. Write a list of those whom you believe highly respect you.

4. Write a list of those from whom you could gain greater respect.

5. How might you gain their respect? List any tools and tactics that you believe would be helpful in doing so.

6. What do you highly respect about yourself?

7. Is there anything that you do not respect about yourself? If so, what are they?

8. Is there a way that you could change that which you do not respect about yourself? If so, how?

9. In regards to action, an effective commander and chief needs to 1) keep his men well organized, 2) drill his men on a regular basis, 3) accustom his body to hardships and 4) understand the terrain that he/she is entering. On a scale from one to ten (one being "not at all" and ten being "a great deal"), rate how well organized you keep those with whom you work:

1——2——3——4——5——6——7——8——9——10

10. What steps can you take to better organize yourself and those who report to you?

11. How often do you drill or test those who report to you? Do you need to do so more often? If so, how frequently?

12. An effective leader should be highly educated about the playing field within which he is embarking. On a scale from one to ten (one being "not at all" and ten being "a great deal"), rate how familiar you are with your playing field:

1——2——3——4——5——6——7——8——9——10

13. What have you already done to familiarize yourself with your current playing field?

14. What steps can you take to better familiarize yourself with your playing field?

15. The author also stipulates that in order to "exercise the intellect" an effective leader should 1) read histories, 2) study the actions of illustrious men and 3) follow the actions of wise and successful leaders before him.

16. How familiar are you with the history of others who have been successful in your area of interest? On a scale from

one to ten (one being "not at all" and ten being "a great deal"), rate how familiar you are with the history of your area of expertise.

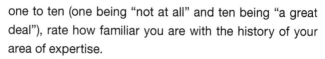

1——2——3——4——5——6——7——8——9——10

17. Have you carefully studied the actions of others who have successfully lead before you? If so, who have you studied? Who would you like to study? Take some time to do so, and write about your findings.

18. *The ability to maintain physical and emotional strength* is the leadership trait listed with this chapter. Is your body in excellent working order? On a scale from one to ten (one being "very unfit" and ten being "in excellent condition"), rate how healthy you are:

1——2——3——4——5——6——7——8——9——10

19. What action steps do you currently take to build your physical strength?

20. What could you do to improve your physical regimen?

21. Are the bodies of those who report to you in excellent working order? On a scale from one to ten (one being "very unfit" and ten being "in excellent condition"), rate how physically fit your team is:

1——2——3——4——5——6——7——8——9——10

22. Do you have any programs or facilities in place to help support your team in improving their physical health?

23. Is your mind in excellent working order? On a scale from one to ten (one being "not very effective" and ten being "in excellent condition"), rate how healthy your mind is:

1——2——3——4——5——6——7——8——9——10

24. What steps can you take to improve your mind (read more books, do puzzles, practice daily mind-enhancing games or exercises, etc.)?

25. Are the minds of those who report to you in excellent working order? On a scale from one to ten (one being "not very effective" and ten being "in excellent condition"), rate how healthy the minds of your staff are:

1——2——3——4——5——6——7——8——9——10

26. What steps can you take to improve their mind (create a library for them, offer lunch classes, have mind-enhancing games, audios or exercises available to them)?

27. Are you emotionally healthy? On a scale from one to ten (one being "not very effective" and ten being "in excellent condition"), rate how emotionally healthy you are:

1——2——3——4——5——6——7——8——9——10

28. What steps have you taken to build your emotional strength? What additional steps might you take to further improve your emotional strength?

29. Is your staff and/or subordinates emotionally healthy? On a scale from one to ten (one being "not very effective" and ten being "in excellent condition"), rate how emotionally healthy they are:

1——2——3——4——5——6——7——8——9——10

30. What steps have you taken to build their emotional strength? What additional steps might you take to further improve their emotional strength (continuous praise, therapy, provide emotional awareness tools like workshops, books, audios, etc.)?

31. Write a list of three steps you can take to improve your overall health (body, mind and emotions). Then be sure to structure these into your routine. Write about any new findings you discover.

Chapter XV

Concerning Things for Which Men, and Especially Princes, Are Praised or Blamed

It remains now to see what ought to be the rules of conduct for a prince towards subject and friends. And as I know that many have written on this point, I expect I shall be considered presumptuous in mentioning it again, especially as in discussing it I shall depart from the methods of other people. But, it being my intention to write a thing which shall be useful to him who apprehends it, it appears to me more appropriate to follow up the real truth of the matter than the imagination of it; for many have pictured republics and principalities which in fact have never been known or seen, because how one lives is so far distant from how one ought to live, that he who neglects what is done for what ought to be done, sooner effects his ruin than his preservation; for a man who wishes to act entirely up to his professions of virtue soon meets with what destroys him among so much that is evil.

Hence it is necessary for a prince wishing to hold his own to know how to do wrong, and to make use of it or not according to necessity. Therefore, putting on one side imaginary things concerning a prince, and discussing those which are real, I say that all men when they are spoken of, and chiefly princes for being more highly placed, are remarkable for some of those qualities which bring them either blame or praise; and thus it is that one is reputed liberal, another miserly, using a Tuscan term (because an avaricious person in our language is still he who desires to possess by robbery, whilst we call one miserly who deprives himself too much of the use of his own); one is reputed generous, one rapacious; one cruel, one compassionate; one faithless, another faithful; one effeminate and cowardly, another bold and brave; one affable, another haughty; one lascivious, another chaste; one sincere, another cunning; one hard, another easy; one grave, another frivolous; one religious, another unbelieving, and the like. And I know that every one will confess that it would be most praiseworthy in a prince to exhibit all the above qualities that are considered good; but because they can neither be entirely possessed nor observed, for human conditions do not permit it, it is necessary for him to be sufficiently prudent that he may know how to avoid the reproach of those vices which would lose him his state; and also to keep himself, if it be possible, from those which would not lose him it; but this not being possible, he may with less hesitation abandon himself to them. And again, he need not make himself uneasy at incurring a reproach for those vices without which the state can only be saved with difficulty, for if everything is considered carefully, it will be found that something which looks like virtue, if followed, would be his ruin; whilst something else, which looks like vice, yet followed brings him security and prosperity.

STUDY GUIDE

Chapter XV

Leadership Trait #15
Endurance—Ability to Remain Energized

The rules of conduct regarding princes (or leaders) are discussed in this chapter. Machiavelli opens with a play on words, stating that learning what not to do is imperative to doing things right. He notes that reality is different than the "How-to" books of etiquette, being that sometimes one has to do the very thing that is suggested they not do when dealing with the real world. He claims that all men, especially those of high visibility (like princes) are *"remarkable for some of those qualities which bring them blame or praise."* Their actions, good or bad are visible and noted by all. He then goes on to list labels—extremes of various personality traits. He then asserts that things are not always as they appear, and that a leader best be aware of both the virtues and the vices. An effective leader needs to know which could empower him and which could cause his ultimate ruin.

Endurance—the ability to remain energized is the leadership trait that this chapter focuses on. While you reflected on the powers that are inherent in strength in the last chapter, endurance is just as essential. Often one can find oneself experiencing bouts of energy and then lack of energy throughout their day. Maintaining your strength and endurance throughout lengthy ordeals puts you a step ahead of the competition when you are building your leadership empire.

1. Is there a code of ethics in the world in which you wish to become successful?

2. Make a list of the "should do's" in that code.

3. Now make a list of the "should not do's" in that code.

4. Are there times when you felt you had to break that code? If so, describe them.

5. What was the outcome of breaking that code?

6. At what points in your leadership initiative do you believe that breaking the code of conduct may be necessary?

7. There is the saying, *"Things aren't always as they appear to be."* Can you think of examples of this in your life?

8. When qualities do you possess that tend to bring shame and blame to you?

9. What qualities are you most noted for that bring you praise?

10. Are there times when apparent virtues have not served you and those you lead? Explain.

11. Are there times when you had to make choices that were lacking in virtue, and you believed them to be for the highest good? Explain.

12. What choices do you believe empower you? List them.

13. Make a list of the choices that you believe could become the ultimate cause of your ruin.

14. The leadership trait associated with this chapter is *endurance—the ability to remain energized.* On a scale from one to ten (one being "not at all" and ten being "a great deal"), rate how much energy you believe you have at the start of your day:

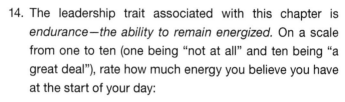

1——2——3——4——5——6——7——8——9——10

15. On a scale from one to ten (one being "not at all" and ten being "a great deal"), rate how much energy you believe you have at the end of your day:

1——2——3——4——5——6——7——8——9——10

16. Especially when in a leadership role, it is important to maintain your energy throughout the day. If you are empathetic in nature, you can become drained by the energetic demands of those around you. Write a list of those activities or interactions with others that drain you.

17. Write a list of the activities or interactions with others than energetically feed you.

18. It is, therefore, imperative to re-energize yourself through-out your day. Do you currently do any practices to ener-gize yourself throughout your day? If so, what are they?

19. Music can be a strong energizer and can shift your atti-tude and focus. Sometimes just listening to a piece of music can raise your energy. Is there any music that does this to you? If so, list the songs, era or type of music that energetically feed you.

20. For many people, getting out in nature can raise their energy frequency. Is this the case with you? If you are not sure, take some time to walk outside at a point where you are feeling fatigued. Note your energy prior to taking the walk, and then after. Do you notice a difference? Has your

energy been raised? If so, take some time to get outdoors each day.

21. Some find cardiovascular workouts, yoga, or other forms of exercise raise their energy. Does any form of exercise raise yours? If so, what forms of exercise?

22. Do you do any such exercise on an ongoing basis? Why or why not?

23. If you haven't already done so, experiment with adding exercise to your daily or weekly routine. Many fitness clubs provide one to two week free trials. If you don't already belong to a club, explore one that is nearby (ideally within 10 minutes of your location), and explore how daily, or weekly exercise affects your energy. Write about your findings.

24. Daily re-energizing exercises such as deep breathing, visualization or meditation can quiet your mind and re-energize you. Do you practice any of these techniques? Explore one or all of these processes, and take note of your findings. If any of them work, be sure to include them in your daily or weekly routine.

25. Schedule at least three daily doses of activities that energize you. Set your alarm each day, so that you will follow through on practicing them. For a month, journal each day about any differences you note after taking time to energetically nourish yourself.

26. Are there any additional practices that you can incorporate into your life that would provide you with greater endurance? If so, list them, and then add them to your ongoing "energizing" routine.

Chapter XVI

Concerning Liberality and Meanness

Commencing then with the first of the above-named characteristics, I say that it would be well to be reputed liberal. Nevertheless, liberality exercised in a way that does not bring you the reputation for it, injures you; for if one exercises it honestly and as it should be exercised, it may not become known, and you will not avoid the reproach of its opposite. Therefore, anyone wishing to maintain among men the name of liberal is obliged to avoid no attribute of magnificence; so that a prince thus inclined will consume in such acts all his property, and will be compelled in the end, if he wish to maintain the name of liberal, to unduly weigh down his people, and tax them, and do every-thing he can to get money. This will soon make him odious to his subjects, and becoming poor he will be little valued by any one; thus, with his liberality, hav-ing offended many and rewarded few, he is affected by the very first trouble and imperiled by whatever may be the first danger; recognizing this himself, and wishing to draw back from it, he runs at once into the reproach of being miserly.

Therefore, a prince, not being able to exercise this virtue of liberality in such a way that it is recognized, except to his cost, if he is wise he ought not to fear the reputation of being mean, for in time he will come to be more considered than if liberal, seeing that with his economy his revenues are enough, that he can defend himself against all attacks, and is able to engage in enterprises without burdening his people; thus it comes to pass that he exercises liberality towards all from whom he does not take, who are numberless, and meanness towards those to whom he does not give, who are few.

We have not seen great things done in our time except by those who have been considered mean; the rest have failed. Pope Julius the Second was assisted in reaching the papacy by a reputation for liberality, yet he did not strive afterwards to keep it up, when he made war on the King of France; and he made many wars without imposing any extraordinary tax on his subjects, for he supplied his additional expenses out of his long thriftiness. The present King of Spain would not have undertaken or conquered in so many enterprises if he had been reputed liberal. A prince, therefore, provided that he has not to rob his subjects, that he can defend himself, that he does not become poor and abject, that he is not forced to become rapacious, ought to hold of little account a reputation for being mean, for it is one of those vices which will enable him to govern.

And if anyone should say: Caesar obtained empire by liberality, and many others have reached the highest positions by having been liberal, and by being considered so, I answer: Either you are a prince in fact, or in a way to become one. In the first case this liberality is dangerous, in the second it is very necessary to be considered liberal; and Caesar was one of those who wished to become preeminent in Rome; but if he had survived after becoming so, and had not moderated his expenses, he would have destroyed his government. And if anyone should reply: Many have been princes, and have done great things with armies, who have been considered very liberal, I reply: Either a prince spends that which is his own or his subjects' or else that of others. In the first case he ought to be sparing, in the second he ought not to neglect any opportunity for liberality. And to the prince who goes forth with his army, supporting it by pillage, sack, and extortion, handling that which belongs to others, this liberality is necessary, otherwise he would not be followed by soldiers. And of that which is neither yours nor your subjects' you can be a ready giver, as were Cyrus, Caesar, and Alexander; because it does not take away your reputation if you squander that of others, but adds to it; it is only squandering your own that injures you.

And there is nothing wastes so rapidly as liberality, for even whilst you exercise it you lose the power to do so, and so become either poor or despised, or else, in avoiding poverty, rapacious and hated. And a prince should guard himself, above all things, against being despised and hated; and liberality leads you to both. Therefore it is wiser to have a reputation for meanness which brings reproach without hatred, than to be compelled through seeking a reputation for liberality to incur a name for rapacity which begets reproach with hatred.

Chapter XVI

Leadership Trait #16
Flexibility—
Ability to Be Malleable and Open to Change

Machiavelli discusses finding the balance between liberality and meanness in this chapter. He opens by stating that one must seek balance, for behaving in a manner too liberal can backfire into situations where one could render the state financially impoverished. In such cases one bears the label of being called a misery, as they would have to then create taxes and other financial stressors on its inhabitants to make up for the loses. He then emphasizes that he has only seen great things from those in his era that were considered mean. He cites several cases, the first being Pope Julius the Second who was considered liberal when seeking his reign, but later was able to fight many battles without imposing taxes on his people because of his thriftiness. He makes a distinction using Caesar as an example, when he states, *"either you are a prince in fact, or in a way to become one."* When you are actually a prince in power, being considered liberal is dangerous, however when you are seeking that position, being considered liberal is necessary. He goes on to state that you only suffer when you squander your riches—whereas squandering that of others boosts your reputation. In the end, he asserts that it is better to be considered mean than a liberal who becomes despised and hated.

Flexibility—Ability to Be Malleable and Open to Change is the leadership trait that you will be focusing on in this chapter. As previously mentioned, even the strongest of trees has to have the ability to move in the wind. An extensive aspect of flexibility involves how well you can adapt to unexpected changes. Developing the stamina and skills to be malleable and able to come up with new and rich strategies in response to unexpected changes is an art and a talent that will take you far in your leadership pursuits.

1. Finding balance between being too liberal or too strict (mean) is imperative to your reputation and success as a leader. On a scale from one to ten (one being "not at all" and ten being "very much"), rate how much balance you have between being considered liberal versus strict.

1——2——3——4——5——6——7——8——9——10

2. How has your liberal nature served you thus far as a respected leader?

3. What choices have you made that you would consider liberal?

4. Have you noted any drawbacks that were the consequence of your more liberal choices? Explain.

5. What were the benefits that came from making such choices?

6. How has your stricter nature served you thus far as a respected leader?

7. What choices have you made that you would consider mean or strict?

8. Have you noted any drawbacks that were the consequence of your more harsh or firm choices? Explain.

9. What were the benefits that came from making such choices?

10. The leadership trait paired with this chapter is *flexibility—the ability to be malleable and open to change.* On a scale from one to ten (one being "not at all" and ten being "a great deal"), rate how flexible you are:

1——2——3——4——5——6——7——8——9——10

11. In what ways are you flexible in your initiatives as a leader?

12. How are you inflexible in your decisions and choices?

13. Do you believe that you have achieved balance? If not, do you believe you need to be more set or more flexible in your ways? Please explain.

14. When one suggests change to you, is your response general enthusiasm or anxiety? Explain.

15. When change is imminent, do you find yourself creatively stimulated? Explain.

16. Are there any action steps you can to achieving more flexibility? List them and follow through on creating an action plan to practice them.

Chapter XVII

Concerning Cruelty and Clemency, and Whether It Is Better To Be Loved Than Feared

Coming now to the other qualities mentioned above, I say that every prince ought to desire to be considered clement and not cruel. Nevertheless he ought to take care not to misuse this clemency. Cesare Borgia was considered cruel; notwithstanding, his cruelty reconciled the Romagna, unified it, and restored it to peace and loyalty. And if this be rightly considered, he will be seen to have been much more merciful than the Florentine people, who, to avoid a reputation for cruelty, permitted Pistoia to be destroyed.* Therefore a prince, so long as he keeps his subjects united and loyal, ought not to mind the reproach of cruelty; because with a few examples he will be more merciful than those who, through too much mercy, allow disorders to arise, from which follow murders or robberies; for these are wont to injure the whole

---

* During the rioting between the Cancellieri and Panciatichi factions in 1502 and 1503.

people, whilst those executions which originate with a prince offend the individual only.

And of all princes, it is impossible for the new prince to avoid the imputation of cruelty, owing to new states being full of dangers. Hence Virgil, through the mouth of Dido, excuses the inhumanity of her reign owing to its being new, saying:

"Res dura, et regni novitas me talia cogun Moliri, et late fines custode tueri."*

Nevertheless he ought to be slow to believe and to act, nor should he himself show fear, but proceed in a temperate manner with prudence and humanity, so that too much confidence may not make him incautious and too much distrust render him intolerable.

Upon this a question arises: whether it be better to be loved than feared or feared than loved? It may be answered that one should wish to be both, but, because it is difficult to unite them in one person, it is much safer to be feared than loved, when, of the two, either must be dispensed with. Because this is to be asserted in general of men, that they are ungrateful, fickle, false, cowardly, covetous, and as long as you succeed they are yours entirely; they will offer you their blood, property, life, and children, as is said above, when the need is far distant; but when it approaches they turn against you. And that prince who, relying entirely on their prom-

---

* . . . *against my will, my fate*
  A throne unsettled, and an infant state,
  Bid me defend my realms with all my pow'rs,
  And guard with these severities my shores.
  —*Christopher Pitt.*

ises, has neglected other precautions, is ruined; because friendships that are obtained by payments, and not by greatness or nobility of mind, may indeed be earned, but they are not secured, and in time of need cannot be relied upon; and men have less scruple in offending one who is beloved than one who is feared, for love is preserved by the link of obligation which, owing to the baseness of men, is broken at every opportunity for their advantage; but fear preserves you by a dread of punishment which never fails.

Nevertheless a prince ought to inspire fear in such a way that, if he does not win love, he avoids hatred; because he can endure very well being feared whilst he is not hated, which will always be as long as he abstains from the property of his citizens and subjects and from their women. But when it is necessary for him to proceed against the life of someone, he must do it on proper justification and for manifest cause, but above all things he must keep his hands off the property of others, because men more quickly forget the death of their father than the loss of their patrimony. Besides, pretexts for taking away the property are never wanting; for he who has once begun to live by robbery will always find pretexts for seizing what belongs to others; but reasons for taking life, on the contrary, are more difficult to find and sooner lapse. But when a prince is with his army, and has under control a multitude of soldiers, then it is quite necessary for him to disregard the reputation of cruelty, for without it he would never hold his army united or disposed to its duties.

Among the wonderful deeds of Hannibal this one is enumerated: that having led an enormous army, composed of many various races of men, to fight in foreign lands, no dissensions arose either among them or against the prince, whether in his bad or in his good fortune. This arose from nothing else than his inhuman cruelty, which, with his boundless valor, made him revered and terrible in the sight of his soldiers, but without that cruelty, his other virtues were not sufficient to produce this effect. And short-sighted writers admire his deeds from one point of view and from another condemn the principal cause of them. That it is true his other virtues would not have been sufficient for him may be proved by the case of Scipio, that most excellent man, not only of his own times but within the memory of man, against whom, nevertheless, his army rebelled in Spain; this arose from nothing but his too great forbearance, which gave his soldiers more license than is consistent with military discipline. For this he was upbraided in the Senate by Fabius Maximus, and called the corrupter of the Roman soldiery. The Locrians were laid waste by a legate of Scipio, yet they were not avenged by him, nor was the insolence of the legate punished, owing entirely to his easy nature. Insomuch that someone in the Senate, wishing to excuse him, said there were many men who knew much better how not to err than to correct the errors of others. This disposition, if he had been continued in the command, would have destroyed in time the fame and glory of Scipio; but, he being under the control of the Senate, this injurious characteristic not only concealed itself, but contributed to his glory.

Returning to the question of being feared or loved, I come to the conclusion that, men loving according to their own will and fearing according to that of the prince, a wise prince should establish himself on that which is in his own control and not in that of others; he must endeavor only to avoid hatred, as is noted.

STUDY GUIDE

Chapter XVII

Leadership Trait #17
Balance—Ability to Maintain Equilibrium

In this chapter Machiavelli discusses the choices between leading with cruelty versus clemency. He opens the chapter suggesting that every prince ought to desire to be considered clement. However, he cites the example of Cesare Borgia who was considered cruel but by being so would have been seen much more merciful than the Florentine people who permitted Pistoia to be destroyed to avoid being considered cruel. A leader's priority should be keeping his or her subjects united and loyal. When a leader is too lenient, violence and disorder can arise. He then quotes Christopher Pitt and shares that there must be balance, where a new leader should avoid showing fear or too much confidence, while proceeding with prudence and humanity. Then in response to the question, *"Is it better to be feared or loved?"* he asserts that one should desire both, however because it is difficult to unite the two, it is better to be feared if one had to choose. While love may create a certain degree of loyalty, Machiavelli suggests that leading by fear can be stronger as your followers' dread of punishment would better keep them in line. A leader may be feared but should avoid being hated, and that includes maintaining a good reputation—steering clear of taking from others' their wives or riches. He then cites two examples. The first being Hannibal as an example of a leader who effectively led a massive, diverse army with cruelty, and claims that he would not have been able to do so without having that trait. The second example being Scipio, an "excellent man" whose army rebelled against him because of his liberal permissiveness. In the end, Machiavelli asserts that one can only control whether others fear you or not. Love can only come from the choices your followers make. Thus it is better to be cruel than clement, as you can then remain in control.

The leadership trait that is affiliated with this chapter is *balance—the ability to maintain equilibrium.* If you are a leader, most likely you are an achiever—someone who strives for success, and performs above and beyond the call of duty. When this is the case, however, you will most likely find yourself burnt out early in your endeavors unless you master the ability to balance your life. Balancing work with recreation, busy time with quiet time, and public time with personal time will assist you in maintaining a well-rounded lifestyle and healthy equilibrium.

1. It is clear throughout this book that Machiavelli asserts than a strong leader has to have the courage to be feared or disliked in order to maintain order. Do you believe this to be so? Explain.

2. Do you consider yourself to be courageous? On a scale from one to ten (one being "not at all" and ten being "very much"), rate courageous you believe yourself to be:

1———2———3———4———5———6———7———8———9———10

3. Provide examples of what you have done that is courageous.

4. Have you had the courage to be disliked by others by making an unpopular decision that you believed was for the highest good? Explain.

5. In this chapter, Machiavelli reflects the tenet of the well-known saying, "You have to be cruel to be kind." Do you believe in this theory? Why or why not? Explain.

6. Research and list any current leaders that you believe have a reputation as being kind, and are successful.

7. Research and list any current leaders that you believe have a reputation as being kind, and are unsuccessful.

8. Research and list any current leaders that you believe have a reputation as being cruel, and are considered successful.

9. Research and list any current leaders that you believe have a reputation as being cruel, and are unsuccessful.

10. Machiavelli asserts that you have control over your followers when you are considered cruel, however you cannot control their love—they can be fickle and turn on you when you are beloved. Describe your thoughts on this theory.

11. Gandhi was a leader after Machiavelli wrote this treatise. He was a very powerful leader who was not considered cruel. How do you believe he plays into this theory, or does he?

12. The leadership trait referenced in this chapter is *balance—the ability to maintain equilibrium.* On a scale from one to ten (one being "not at all" and ten being "a great deal"), rate how balanced you believe yourself to be:

1——2——3——4——5——6——7——8——9——10

13. In what ways do you considered yourself balanced?

14. List the ways in which you are imbalanced.

15. What steps can you take to gain equilibrium in your life?

16. How does imbalance show up in your efforts to become a successful leader?

17. Why is balance important in leadership?

18. What is the outcome that arises from imbalance in leadership? Explain.

19. Many would say that the energy of a people trickles down from the top to the bottom. In other words, if a leader is not balanced, he causes this among his followers. What are your thoughts and beliefs on this? Explain.

20. What three steps can you take to gain further balance in your life and in your leadership initiatives? List them, and then set a deadline upon which you will implement these initiatives.

Chapter XVIII

Concerning the Way in Which Princes Should Keep Faith[*]

Every one admits how praiseworthy it is in a prince to keep faith, and to live with integrity and not with craft. Nevertheless our experience has been that those princes who have done great things have held good faith of little account, and have known how to circumvent the intellect of men by craft, and in the end have overcome those who have relied on their word. You must know there are two ways of contesting,[†] the one by the law, the other by force; the first method is proper to men, the second to beasts; but because the first is frequently not sufficient, it is necessary to have recourse

---

[*] "The present chapter has given greater offence than any other portion of Machiavelli's writings." —Burd, "Il Principe," p. 297.

[†] "Contesting," i.e. "striving for mastery." Mr Burd points out that this passage is imitated directly from Cicero's "De Officiis": "Nam cum sint duo genera decertandi, unum per disceptationem, alterum per vim; cumque illud proprium sit hominis, hoc beluarum; confugiendum est ad posterius, si uti non licet superiore."

to the second. Therefore it is necessary for a prince to understand how to avail himself of the beast and the man. This has been figuratively taught to princes by ancient writers, who describe how Achilles and many other princes of old were given to the Centaur Chiron to nurse, who brought them up in his discipline; which means solely that, as they had for a teacher one who was half beast and half man, so it is necessary for a prince to know how to make use of both natures, and that one without the other is not durable. A prince, therefore, being compelled knowingly to adopt the beast, ought to choose the fox and the lion; because the lion cannot defend himself against snares and the fox cannot defend himself against wolves. Therefore, it is necessary to be a fox to discover the snares and a lion to terrify the wolves. Those who rely simply on the lion do not understand what they are about. Therefore a wise lord cannot, nor ought he to, keep faith when such observance may be turned against him, and when the reasons that caused him to pledge it exist no longer. If men were entirely good this precept would not hold, but because they are bad, and will not keep faith with you, you too are not bound to observe it with them. Nor will there ever be wanting to a prince legitimate reasons to excuse this non-observance. Of this, endless modern examples could be given, showing how many treaties and engagements have been made void and of no effect through the faithlessness of princes; and he who has known best how to employ the fox has succeeded best.

But it is necessary to know well how to disguise this characteristic, and to be a great pretender and dissembler; and men are so simple, and so subject to present necessities, that he who seeks to deceive will always find someone who will allow himself to be deceived. One recent example I cannot pass over in silence. Alexander the Sixth did nothing else but deceive men, nor ever thought of doing otherwise, and he always found victims; for there never was a man who had greater power in asserting, or who with greater oaths would affirm a thing, yet would observe it less; nevertheless his deceits always succeeded according to his wishes,* because he well understood this side of mankind.

Alexander never did what he said,
Cesare never said what he did.
—Italian Proverb.

Therefore it is unnecessary for a prince to have all the good qualities I have enumerated, but it is very necessary to appear to have them. And I shall dare to say this also, that to have them and always to observe them is injurious, and that to appear to have them is useful; to appear merciful, faithful, humane, religious, upright, and to be so, but with a mind so framed that should you require not to be so, you may be able and know how to change to the opposite.

---

* "Nondimanco sempre gli succederono gli inganni (ad votum)." The words "ad votum" are omitted in the Testina addition, 1550.

And you have to understand this, that a prince, especially a new one, cannot observe all those things for which men are esteemed, being often forced, in order to maintain the state, to act contrary to fidelity,* friendship, humanity, and religion. Therefore it is necessary for him to have a mind ready to turn itself accordingly as the winds and variations of fortune force it, yet, as I have said above, not to diverge from the good if he can avoid doing so, but, if compelled, then to know how to set about it.

For this reason a prince ought to take care that he never lets anything slip from his lips that is not replete with the above-named five qualities, that he may appear to him who sees and hears him altogether merciful, faithful, humane, upright, and religious. There is nothing more necessary to appear to have than this last quality, inasmuch as men judge generally more by the eye than by the hand, because it belongs to everybody to see you, to few to come in touch with you. Everyone sees what you appear to be, few really know what you are, and those few dare not oppose themselves to the opinion of the many, who have the majesty of the state to defend

---

* "Contrary to fidelity" or "faith," "contro alla fede, and "tutto fede," "altogether faithful," in the next paragraph. It is noteworthy that these two phrases, "contro alla fede" and "tutto fede," were omitted in the Testina edition, which was published with the sanction of the papal authorities. It may be that the meaning attached to the word "fede" was "the faith," i.e. the Catholic creed, and not as rendered here "fidelity" and "faithful." Observe that the word "religione" was suffered to stand in the text of the Testina, being used to signify indifferently every shade of belief, as witness "the religion," a phrase inevitably employed to designate the Huguenot heresy. South in his Sermon IX, p. 69, ed. 1843, comments on this passage as follows: "That great patron and Coryphaeus of this tribe, Niccolo Machiavel, laid down this for a master rule in his political scheme: 'That the show of religion was helpful to the politician, but the reality of it hurtful and pernicious.'"

them; and in the actions of all men, and especially of princes, which it is not prudent to challenge, one judges by the result.

For that reason, let a prince have the credit of conquering and holding his state, the means will always be considered honest, and he will be praised by everybody; because the vulgar are always taken by what a thing seems to be and by what comes of it; and in the world there are only the vulgar, for the few find a place there only when the many have no ground to rest on.

One prince* of the present time, whom it is not well to name, never preaches anything else but peace and good faith, and to both he is most hostile, and either, if he had kept it, would have deprived him of reputation and kingdom many a time.

---

* Ferdinand of Aragon. "When Machiavelli was writing 'The Prince' it would have been clearly impossible to mention Ferdinand's name here without giving offence." Burd's "Il Principe," p. 308.

STUDY GUIDE

Chapter XVIII

Leadership Trait #18:
Nourishment—
Ability to Absorb Energetic Nourishment

This chapter of *The Prince* has been considered by many as the most offensive in the book. While Machiavelli states that maintaining faith is praiseworthy in a leader, the most effective leaders have been so because they are crafty, and can circumvent the intellect of their enemies and followers. He explains that there are two ways of contesting. The first is by law and the second, by force. He brings the story of Achilles into the treatise as an example of a leader who was raised by a half-breast, emphasizing that a good leader needs to embody both man and beast to be successful. He suggests that a wise leader choose the fox and lion as the beasts that he or she emulates. Each has their weaknesses, however using the cunning of the fox and the might of the lion. It is likely that what many take great offense to in this chapter is Machiavelli's assertion that man is not good by nature. He then goes on to assert that one also needs to be a great deceiver, citing Alexander the Sixth as a leader who successfully did so. While an effective leader may not have all of the qualities Machiavelli outlines in this text, he states that it is important that good leaders "appear" to have them.

The ability to absorb energetic nourishment is the leadership trait that we will reflect on in this chapter. While food provides nourishment, many other factors affect your energy and can either nourish or deplete your energy. Being a leader, you are very often a public figure, thus it is important that you pay attention to your energy. You should encourage that which energetically supports you and protect yourself from individuals or circumstances that energetically drain you. The first step is to become aware of your energy and the energy of those around you.

1. Machiavelli asserts that while having faith in your followers is important, a good leader must also be crafty and able to circumvent the intellect of men. In such cases, in order to affect the intellect of one's followers, a crafty leader should be intelligent, quick-witted and very convincing. On a scale from one to ten (one being "not at all" and ten being "a great deal"), rate how intelligent you believe yourself to be:

1——2——3——4——5——6——7——8——9——10

2. Do you think you are intelligent enough to be an effective leader? Why or why not?

3. If you feel you need more intelligence, are there practices you can incorporate into your life that would raise your I.Q.?

4. On a scale from one to ten (one being "not at all" and ten being "a great deal"), rate quick-witted you believe yourself to be:

1——2——3——4——5——6——7——8——9——10

5. How do you demonstrate your quick-wittedness?

6. How does being quick-witted assist you with your leadership initiatives?

7. Do you think you need to be more quick-witted? If so, how can you strengthen this skill?

8. On a scale from one to ten (one being "not at all" and ten being "a great deal"), rate how convincing you believe yourself to be:

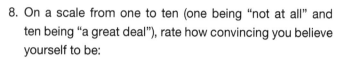

9. As a leader, what initiatives do you have where you would need to use this skill?

10. Have you ever practiced formal debating? Do you think that doing so would heighten your ability to be convincing? What other things could you do to improve upon your ability to be convincing with others?

11. The leadership trait that is listed with this chapter is *the ability to nourish yourself energetically*. Do you believe you are effective at doing so? On a scale from one to ten (one being "not at all" and ten being "a great deal"), rate effective you are an energetically nourishing yourself:

12. What do you do to energize yourself?

13. How do you nourish your mind?

14. What can you further do to nourish your mind?

15. On a scale from one to ten (one being "not at all" and ten being "very much so"), rate effective you are at nourishing your soul:

16. What nourishes your soul?

17. Are there any steps you can take to further nourishing your soul? If so what are they? Make an action plan to start including them in your daily, weekly or monthly routine.

18. How do you nourish your body?

19. On a scale from one to ten (one being "not at all" and ten being "very much so"), rate effective you are at nourishing your body:

1——2——3——4——5——6——7——8——9——10

20. What steps can you take to further nourish your body?

21. Expressing gratitude for the food you eat and your good health can increase your energy. Do you believe this to be true? Why or why not?

22. Do you express gratitude? Why or why not? Explain.

23. If you believe that an attitude of gratitude will increase your energy and enhance your life, write out a gratitude plan and follow through with it.

24. List three things that most deplete you of energy.

25. What can you do to protect yourself from energy depletion?

26. List three things that best feed you energetically.

27. What steps can you take to further feed yourself energetically?

Chapter XIX

That One Should Avoid
Being Despised and Hated

Now, concerning the characteristics of which mention is made above, I have spoken of the more important ones, the others I wish to discuss briefly under this generality, that the prince must consider, as has been in part said before, how to avoid those things which will make him hated or contemptible; and as often as he shall have succeeded he will have fulfilled his part, and he need not fear any danger in other reproaches.

It makes him hated above all things, as I have said, to be rapacious, and to be a violator of the property and women of his subjects, from both of which he must abstain. And when neither their property nor their honor is touched, the majority of men live content, and he has only to contend with the ambition of a few, whom he can curb with ease in many ways.

It makes him contemptible to be considered fickle, frivolous, effeminate, mean-spirited, irresolute, from all of which a prince should guard himself as from a rock; and he should endeavor to show in his actions greatness, courage, gravity, and fortitude; and in his private dealings with his subjects let him show that his judgments are irrevocable, and maintain himself in such reputation that no one can hope either to deceive him or to get round him.

That prince is highly esteemed who conveys this impression of himself, and he who is highly esteemed is not easily conspired against; for, provided it is well known that he is an excellent man and revered by his people, he can only be attacked with difficulty. For this reason a prince ought to have two fears, one from within, on account of his subjects, the other from without, on account of external powers. From the latter he is defended by being well armed and having good allies, and if he is well armed he will have good friends, and affairs will always remain quiet within when they are quiet without, unless they should have been already disturbed by conspiracy; and even should affairs outside be disturbed, if he has carried out his preparations and has lived as I have said, as long as he does not despair, he will resist every attack, as I said Nabis the Spartan did.

But concerning his subjects, when affairs outside are disturbed he has only to fear that they will conspire secretly, from which a prince can easily secure himself by avoiding being hated and despised, and by keeping the people satisfied with him, which it is most necessary for him to accomplish, as I said above at length. And one of the most efficacious remedies that a prince can have against conspiracies is not to be hated and despised by the people, for he who conspires against a prince always expects to please them by his removal; but when the conspirator can only look forward to offending them, he will not have the courage to take such a course, for the difficulties that confront a conspirator are infinite. And as experience shows, many have been the conspiracies, but few have been successful; because he who conspires cannot act alone, nor can he take a companion except from those whom he believes to be malcontents, and as soon as you have opened your mind to a malcontent you have given him the material with which to content himself, for by denouncing you he can look for every advantage; so that, seeing the gain from this course to be assured, and seeing the other to be doubtful and full of dangers, he must be a very rare friend, or a thoroughly obstinate enemy of the prince, to keep faith with you.

And, to reduce the matter into a small compass, I say that, on the side of the conspirator, there is nothing but fear, jealousy, prospect of punishment to terrify him; but on the side of the prince there is the majesty of the principality, the laws, the protection of friends and the state to defend him; so that, adding to all these things the popular goodwill, it is impossible that any one should be so rash as to conspire. For whereas in general the conspirator has to fear before the execution of his plot, in this case he has also to fear the sequel to the crime; because on account of it he has the people for an enemy, and thus cannot hope for any escape.

Endless examples could be given on this subject, but I will be content with one, brought to pass within the memory of our fathers. Messer Annibale Bentivogli, who was prince in Bologna (grandfather of the present Annibale), having been murdered by the Canneschi, who had conspired against him, not one of his family survived but Messer Giovanni,* who was in childhood: immediately after his assassination the people rose and murdered all the Canneschi. This sprung from the popular goodwill which the house of Bentivogli enjoyed in those days in Bologna; which was so great that, although none remained there after the death of Annibale who was able to rule the state, the Bolognese, having information that there was one of the Bentivogli family in Florence, who up to that time had been considered the son of a blacksmith, sent to Florence for him and gave him the government of their city, and it was ruled by him until Messer Giovanni came in due course to the government.

For this reason I consider that a prince ought to reckon conspiracies of little account when his people hold him in esteem; but when it is hostile to him, and bears hatred towards him, he ought to fear everything and everybody. And well- ordered states and wise princes have taken every care not to drive the nobles to desperation, and to keep the people satisfied and contented, for this is one of the most important objects a prince can have.

Among the best ordered and governed kingdoms of our times is France, and in it are found many good institutions on which depend the liberty and security of the king; of these the first is the parliament and its authority, because he who founded the kingdom, knowing the am-

---

* Giovanni Bentivogli, born in Bologna 1438, died at Milan 1508. He ruled Bologna from 1462 to 1506. Machiavelli's strong condemnation of conspiracies may get its edge from his own very recent experience (February 1513), when he had been arrested and tortured for his alleged complicity in the Boscoli conspiracy.

bition of the nobility and their boldness, considered that a bit to their mouths would be necessary to hold them in; and, on the other side, knowing the hatred of the people, founded in fear, against the nobles, he wished to protect them, yet he was not anxious for this to be the particular care of the king; therefore, to take away the reproach which he would be liable to from the nobles for favoring the people, and from the people for favoring the nobles, he set up an arbiter, who should be one who could beat down the great and favor the lesser without reproach to the king. Neither could you have a better or a more prudent arrangement, or a greater source of security to the king and kingdom. From this one can draw another important conclusion, that princes ought to leave affairs of reproach to the management of others, and keep those of grace in their own hands. And further, I consider that a prince ought to cherish the nobles, but not so as to make himself hated by the people.

It may appear, perhaps, to some who have examined the lives and deaths of the Roman emperors that many of them would be an example contrary to my opinion, seeing that some of them lived nobly and showed great qualities of soul, nevertheless they have lost their empire or have been killed by subjects who have conspired against them. Wishing, therefore, to answer these objections, I will recall the characters of some of the emperors, and will show that the causes of their ruin were not different to those alleged by me; at the same time I will only submit for consideration those things that are noteworthy to him who studies the affairs of those times.

It seems to me sufficient to take all those emperors who succeeded to the empire from Marcus the philosopher down to Maximinus; they were Marcus and his son Commodus, Pertinax, Julian, Severus and his son Antoninus Caracalla, Macrinus, Heliogabalus, Alexander, and Maximinus.

There is first to note that, whereas in other principalities the ambition of the nobles and the insolence of the people only have to be contended with, the Roman emperors had a third difficulty in having to put up with the cruelty and avarice of their soldiers, a matter so beset with difficulties that it was the ruin of many; for it was a hard thing to give satisfaction both to soldiers and people; because the people loved peace, and for this reason they loved the unaspiring prince, whilst the soldiers loved the warlike prince who was bold, cruel, and rapacious, which qualities they were quite willing he should exercise upon the people, so that they could get double pay and give vent to their own greed and cruelty. Hence it arose that those emperors were always overthrown who, either by birth or training, had no great authority, and most of them, especially those who came new to the principality, recognizing the difficulty of these two opposing humours, were inclined to give satisfaction to the soldiers, caring little about injuring the people. Which course was necessary, because, as princes cannot help being hated by someone, they ought, in the first place, to avoid being hated by every one, and when they cannot compass this, they ought to endeavour with the utmost diligence to avoid the hatred of the most powerful. Therefore, those emperors who through inexperience had need of special favor adhered more readily to the soldiers than to the people; a course which turned out advantageous to them or not, accordingly as the prince knew how to maintain authority over them.

From these causes it arose that Marcus, Pertinax, and Alexander, being all men of modest life, lovers of justice, enemies to cruelty, humane, and benignant, came to a sad end except Marcus; he alone lived and died honored, because he had succeeded to the throne by hereditary title, and owed nothing either to the soldiers or the people; and afterwards, being possessed of many virtues which made him respected, he always kept both orders in their places whilst he lived, and was neither hated nor despised.

But Pertinax was created emperor against the wishes of the soldiers, who, being accustomed to live licentiously under Commodus, could not endure the honest life to which Pertinax wished to reduce them; thus, having given cause for hatred, to which hatred there was added contempt for his old age, he was overthrown at the very beginning of his administration. And here it should be noted that hatred is acquired as much by good works as by bad ones, therefore, as I said before, a prince wishing to keep his state is very often forced to do evil; for when that body is corrupt whom you think you have need of to maintain yourself—it may be either the people or the soldiers or the nobles—you have to submit to its humours and to gratify them, and then good works will do you harm.

But let us come to Alexander, who was a man of such great goodness, that among the other praises which are accorded him is this, that in the fourteen years he held the empire no one was ever put to death by him unjudged; nevertheless, being considered effeminate and a man who allowed himself to be governed by his mother, he became despised, the army conspired against him, and murdered him.

Turning now to the opposite characters of Commodus, Severus, Antoninus Caracalla, and Maximinus, you will find them all cruel and rapacious-men who, to satisfy their soldiers, did not hesitate to commit every kind of iniquity against the people; and all, except Severus, came to a bad end; but in Severus there was so much valor that, keeping the soldiers friendly, although the people were oppressed by him, he reigned successfully; for his valor made him so much admired in the sight of the soldiers and people that the latter were kept in a way astonished and awed and the former respectful and satisfied. And because the actions of this man, as a new prince, were great, I wish to show briefly that he knew well how to counterfeit the fox and the lion, which natures, as I said above, it is necessary for a prince to imitate.

Knowing the sloth of the Emperor Julian, he persuaded the army in Sclavonia, of which he was captain, that it would be right to go to Rome and avenge the death of Pertinax, who had been killed by the praetorian soldiers; and under this pretext, without appearing to aspire to the throne, he moved the army on Rome, and reached Italy before it was known that he had started. On his arrival at Rome, the Senate, through fear, elected him emperor and killed Julian. After this there remained for Severus, who wished to make himself master of the whole empire, two difficulties; one in Asia, where Niger, head of the Asiatic army, had caused himself to be proclaimed emperor; the other in the west where Albinus was, who also aspired to the throne. And as he considered it dangerous to declare himself hostile to both, he decided to attack Niger and to deceive Albinus. To the latter he wrote that, being elected emperor by the Senate, he was willing to share that dignity with him and sent him the title of Caesar; and, moreover, that the Senate had made Albinus his colleague; which things were accepted by Albinusas true. But after Severus had conquered and killed Niger, and settled oriental affairs, he returned to Rome and complained to the Senate that Albinus, little recognizing the benefits that he had received from him, had by treachery sought to murder him, and for this ingratitude he was compelled to punish him.

Afterwards he sought him out in France, and took from him his government and life. He who will, therefore, carefully examine the actions of this man will find him a most valiant lion and a most cunning fox; he will find him feared and respected by everyone, and not hated by the army; and it need not be wondered at that he, a new man, was able to hold the empire so well, because his supreme renown always protected him from that hatred which the people might have conceived against him for his violence.

But his son Antoninus was a most eminent man, and had very excellent qualities, which made him admirable in the sight of the people and acceptable to the soldiers, for he was a warlike man, most enduring of fatigue, a despiser of all delicate food and other luxuries, which caused him to be beloved by the armies. Nevertheless, his ferocity and cruelties were so great and so unheard of that, after endless single murders, he killed a large number of the people of Rome and all those of Alexandria. He became hated by the whole world, and also feared by those he had around him, to such an extent that he was murdered in the midst of his army by a centurion. And here it must be noted that such-like deaths, which are deliberately inflicted with a resolved and desperate courage, cannot be avoided by princes, because anyone who does not fear to die can inflict them; but a prince may fear them the less because they are very rare; he has only to be careful not to do any grave injury to those whom he employs or has around him in the service of the state. Antoninus had not taken this care, but had contumeliously killed a brother of that centurion, whom also he daily threatened, yet retained in his bodyguard; which, as it turned out, was a rash thing to do, and proved the emperor's ruin.

But let us come to Commodus, to whom it should have been very easy to hold the empire, for, being the son of Marcus, he had inherited it, and he had only to follow in the footsteps of his father to please his people and soldiers; but, being by nature cruel and brutal, he gave himself up to amusing the soldiers and corrupting them, so that he might indulge his rapacity upon the people; on the other hand, not maintaining his dignity, often descending to the theatre to compete with gladiators, and doing other vile things, little worthy of the imperial majesty, he fell into contempt with the soldiers, and being hated by one party and despised by the other, he was conspired against and was killed.

It remains to discuss the character of Maximinus. He was a very warlike man, and the armies, being disgusted with the effeminacy of Alexander, of whom I have already spoken, killed him and elected Maximinus to the throne. This he did not possess for long, for two things made him hated and despised; the one, his having kept sheep in Thrace, which brought him into contempt (it being well known to all, and considered a great indignity by every one), and the other, his having at the accession to his dominions deferred going to Rome and taking possession of the imperial seat; he had also gained a reputation for the utmost ferocity by having, through his prefects in Rome and elsewhere in the empire, practiced many cruelties, so that the whole world was moved to anger at the meanness of his birth and to fear at his barbarity. First Africa rebelled, then the Senate with all the people of Rome, and all Italy conspired against him, to which may be added his own army; this latter, besieging Aquileia and meeting with difficulties in taking it, were disgusted with his cruelties, and fearing him less when they found so many against him, murdered him.

I do not wish to discuss Heliogabalus, Macrinus, or Julian, who, being thoroughly contemptible, were quickly wiped out; but I will bring this discourse to a conclusion by saying that princes in our times have this difficulty of giving inordinate satisfaction to their soldiers in a far less degree, because, notwithstanding one has to give them some indulgence, that is soon done; none of these princes have armies that are veterans in the governance and administration of provinces, as were the armies of the Roman Empire; and whereas it was then more necessary to give satisfaction to the soldiers than to the people, it is now more necessary to all princes, except the Turk and the Soldan, to satisfy the people rather the soldiers, because the people are the more powerful.

From the above I have excepted the Turk, who always keeps round him twelve thousand infantry and fifteen thousand cavalry on which depend the security and strength of the kingdom, and it is necessary that, putting aside every consideration for the people, he should keep them his friends. The kingdom of the Soldan is similar; being entirely in the hands of soldiers, it follows again that, without regard to the people, he must keep them his friends. But you must note that the state of the Soldan is unlike all other principalities, for the reason that it is like the Christian pontificate, which cannot be called either an hereditary or a newly formed principality; because the sons of the old prince are not the heirs, but he who is elected to that position by those who have authority, and the sons remain only noblemen. And this being an ancient custom, it cannot be called a new principality, because there are none of those difficulties in it that are met with in new ones; for although the prince is new, the constitution of the state is old, and it is framed so as to receive him as if he were its hereditary lord.

But returning to the subject of our discourse, I say that whoever will consider it will acknowledge that either hatred or contempt has been fatal to the above-named emperors, and it will be recognized also how it happened that, a number of them acting in one way and a number in another, only one in each way came to a happy end and the rest to unhappy ones. Because it would have been useless and dangerous for Pertinax and Alexander, being new princes, to imitate Marcus, who was heir to the principality; and likewise it would have been utterly destructive to Caracalla, Commodus, and Maximinus to have imitated Severus, they not having sufficient valor to enable them to tread in his footsteps. Therefore a prince, new to the principality, cannot imitate the actions of Marcus, nor, again, is it necessary to follow those of Severus, but he ought to take from Severus those parts which are necessary to found his state, and from Marcus those which are proper and glorious to keep a state that may already be stable and firm.

STUDY GUIDE

Chapter XIX

Leadership Trait #19
Inspiration—
the Ability to Stir the Souls of Your Followers

At the beginning of this chapter, Machiavelli re-asserts a wise leader avoids the properties and women of his subjects. He then states that to be considered any of the following traits makes a leader contemptible: fickle, frivolous, effeminate, mean-spirited, and irresolute. He maintains that an effective leader should endeavor to show in his or her actions: greatness, courage, gravity, fortitude and irrevocability. Citing Nabis the Spartan, Machiavelli declares that a highly esteemed leader is not easily conspired against. Leaders should have two fears of upheavals: one from within with his subjects, and the other from external powers. In both cases, if leaders follow Machiavelli's suggestions, he should remain quite secure. He asserts that conspirators of popular leaders rarely succeed, because they cannot rebel alone and must gain confidence in others. However, if others are malcontent of the existing leader, chances are they have their own agendas and are not to be trusted. The only arms a conspirator has are fear, jealousy and potential punishment; however the leader has the principality, laws, the state and friends to support him. Machiavelli cites the Canneschi's murder of the prince of Bologna as an example of a failed conspiratorial uprising. Ultimately the conspirators failed.

Maintaining a place of high esteem and popularity among one's followers should be one of the most important initiatives of a leader. The leader of France wisely hired an arbiter to alleviate grievances between nobility and the masses. Ideally this was an example of leaving issues of reproach to others.

Referencing all emperors from Marcus the philosopher to Maximinus, Machiavelli asserts the Roman Empire was an example of unrest because the people wanted peace and the soldiers revered a warlike prince. He makes a point with Pertinax, whereby he entered into reign in a kingdom that was corrupt. Machiavelli asserts that entering into such conditions; the leader has to be evil to override such conditions. He then cites Alexander as being effeminate was ultimately murdered. He then turns to discuss the characters of Commodus, Severus, Antoninus, Caracalla and Maximinus, all of whom were "cruel and rapacious" men. With the exception of Severus, each of these leaders "came to a bad end." Machiavelli hails Severus as having embodied the valiance of the lion and the cunning of the fox. He was feared and respected by everyone and not hated by his army. From the Barbary of Antoninus to the brutality of Marcus's on, Commodus and Alexander's successor, Maximinus, Machiavelli provides one example after another of cruel leaders who fell from power and grace because of their evil nature. In the end, he emphasizes that a wise leader will learn from the best of the best before him or her.

The leadership trait that is reflected upon in this chapter is *inspiration—the ability to stir the souls of your followers.* All outstanding leaders have the ability to emotionally move their followers. While charisma may draw the masses to you, you are sure to gain the deepest loyalty and support when you are able to touch others from the heart, and at the deepest level. To stir the hearts of others, yours must first be stirred. Passion and deeply felt inspiration are the magnets and the might that move nations.

1. According to Machiavelli, contemptible leaders have the following traits: fickle, frivolous, effeminate, mean-spirited, and irresolute. Are there any traits that you disagree with in this list? Why or why not?

2. Are there any additional contemptible traits that you would add to your list? If so, what are they and why do you believe they are not indicative of great leaders.

3. On a scale from one to ten (one being "not at all" and ten being "a great deal"), rate how fickle you believe yourself to be:

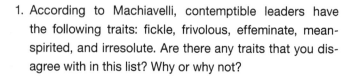

1——2——3——4——5——6——7——8——9——10

4. In what ways are you fickle?

5. How does being fickle interfere with your leadership initiatives?

6. What action steps can you take to be more assertive and firm?

7. On a scale from one to ten (one being "not at all" and ten being "a great deal"), rate how frivolous you are:

1——2——3——4——5——6——7——8——9——10

8. In what ways do you consider yourself frivolous?

9. What action steps can you take to become less frivolous?

10. When Machiavelli references individuals as "effeminate," he discusses how such leaders rely upon the instructions of their mothers. For the purposes of this course, we will focus on how much you rely on the advice of others when making decisions. On a scale from one to ten (one being "not at all" and ten being "a great deal"), rate how much you require input from others when making decisions:

1——2——3——4——5——6——7——8——9——10

11. Why do you think you need support from others when making decisions?

12. Do you believe that seeking the advice of others is detrimental or beneficial when making decisions? Please explain.

13. What action steps could you take towards becoming more independent in your decision-making? Write a list of options, and follow through on them. Then write any changes you note when doing so.

14. Machiavelli asserts that an effective leader should endeavor to show in his or her actions: greatness, courage, gravity, fortitude and irrevocability. On a scale from one to ten (one being "not at all" and ten being "a great deal"), rate how your actions exemplify a sense of "greatness":

1——2——3——4——5——6——7——8——9——10

15. In what ways do you carry "greatness" as a leader?

16. On a scale from one to ten (one being "not at all" and ten being "a great deal"), rate much courage you have:

1——2——3——4——5——6——7——8——9——10

17. Define what you believe courage to be, and explain why.

18. List the ways in which you have been courageous in your life.

19. List the times where you believe you could have been more courageous in your life.

20. What would a courageous leader look like to you?

21. What action steps can you take to become more courageous in your life?

22. On a scale from one to ten (one being "not at all" and ten being "a great deal"), rate much gravity you have:

1——2——3——4——5——6——7——8——9——10

23. What actions would a leader who possessed gravity take to support their initiatives?

24. What steps can you take to gain more gravity in your leadership initiatives?

25. On a scale from one to ten (one being "not at all" and ten being "a great deal"), rate much fortitude you have:

1——2——3——4——5——6——7——8——9——10

26. During what times in your life have you given up on something, and not had the fortitude to see it through? What was the outcome?

27. What steps can you take to gain more fortitude when times get rough?

28. On a scale from one to ten (one being "not at all" and ten being "a great deal"), rate much irrevocability you have:

1——2——3——4——5——6——7——8——9——10

29. Some find making big decisions easy, and are indecisive with small ones. Others are the opposite. In what kinds of decisions do you find yourself indecisive?

30. What action steps can you take to become more decisive in your life?

31. The leadership trait listed with this chapter is *inspiration— the ability to stir the souls of your followers*. On a scale from one to ten (one being "not at all" and ten being "a great deal"), rate how inspiring you believe yourself to be:

1——2——3——4——5——6——7——8——9——10

32. Are you interested in inspiring others? Why or why not?

33. How do you currently inspire others?

34. What steps can you take to develop your ability to inspire others? What initiatives can you take to further inspire others?

35. Research someone who is an inspiring leader. Study them, noting what they did to inspire others. Make a list of the ways in which they moved others, and then see if you can implement their techniques using your own unique style to do so.

36. If you are not interested in inspiring others, perhaps you can find someone who is inspiring and supports your leadership initiatives. Then be sure to contact them and see if they would be willing to support your leadership initiatives.

Chapter XX

Are Fortresses, and Many Other Things To Which Princes Often Resort, Advantageous or Hurtful?

1. Some princes, so as to hold securely the state, have disarmed their subjects; others have kept their subject towns distracted by factions; others have fostered enmities against themselves; others have laid themselves out to gain over those whom they distrusted in the beginning of their governments; some have built fortresses; some have overthrown and destroyed them. And although one cannot give a final judgment on all of these things unless one possesses the particulars of those states in which a decision has to be made, nevertheless I will speak as comprehensively as the matter of itself will admit.

2. There never was a new prince who has disarmed his subjects; rather when he has found them disarmed he has always armed them, because, by arming them, those arms become yours, those

men who were distrusted become faithful, and those who were faithful are kept so, and your subjects become your adherents. And whereas all subjects cannot be armed, yet when those whom you do arm are benefited, the others can be handled more freely, and this difference in their treatment, which they quite understand, makes the former your dependents, and the latter, considering it to be necessary that those who have the most danger and service should have the most reward, excuse you. But when you disarm them, you at once offend them by showing that you distrust them, either for cowardice or for want of loyalty, and either of these opinions breeds hatred against you. And because you cannot remain unarmed, it follows that you turn to mercenaries, which are of the character already shown; even if they should be good they would not be sufficient to defend you against powerful enemies and distrusted subjects. Therefore, as I have said, a new prince in a new principality has always distributed arms. Histories are full of examples. But when a prince acquires a new state, which he adds as a province to his old one, then it is necessary to disarm the men of that state, except those who have been his adherents in acquiring it; and these again, with time and opportunity, should be rendered soft and effeminate; and matters should be managed in such a way that all the armed men in the state shall be your own soldiers who in your old state were living near you.

3. Our forefathers, and those who were reckoned wise, were accustomed to say that it was necessary to hold Pistoia by factions and Pisa by fortresses; and with this idea they fostered quarrels in some of their tributary towns so as to keep possession of them the more easily. This may have been well enough in those times when Italy was in a way balanced, but I do not believe that it can be accepted as a precept for to-day, because I do not believe that factions can ever be of use; rather it is certain that when the enemy comes upon you in divided cities you are quickly lost, because the weakest party will always assist the outside forces and the other will not be able to resist. The Venetians, moved, as I believe, by the above reasons, fostered the Guelph and Ghibelline factions in their tributary cities; and although they never allowed them to come to bloodshed, yet they nursed these disputes amongst them, so that the citizens, distracted by their differences, should not unite against them. Which, as we saw, did not afterwards turn out as expected, because, after the rout at Vaila, one party at once took courage and seized the state. Such methods argue, therefore, weakness in the prince, because these factions will never be permitted in a vigorous principality; such methods for enabling one the more easily to manage subjects are only useful in times of peace, but if war comes this policy proves fallacious.

4. Without doubt princes become great when they overcome the difficulties and obstacles by which they are confronted, and therefore fortune, especially when she desires to make a new prince great, who has a greater necessity to earn renown than an hereditary one, causes enemies to arise and form designs against him, in order that he may have the opportunity of overcoming them, and by them to mount higher, as by a ladder which his enemies have raised. For this reason many consider that a wise prince, when he has the opportunity, ought with craft to foster some animosity against himself, so that, having crushed it, his renown may rise higher.

5. Princes, especially new ones, have found more fidelity and assistance in those men who in the beginning of their rule were distrusted than among those who in the beginning were trusted. Pandolfo Petrucci, Prince of Siena, ruled his state more by those who had been distrusted than by others. But on this question one cannot speak generally, for it varies so much with the individual; I will only say this, that those men who at the commencement of a princedom have been hostile, if they are of a description to need assistance to support themselves, can always be gained over with the greatest ease, and they will be tightly held to serve the prince with fidelity, inasmuch as they know it to be very necessary for them to cancel by deeds the bad impression which he had formed of them; and thus the prince

always extracts more profit from them than from those who, serving him in too much security, may neglect his affairs. And since the matter demands it, I must not fail to warn a prince, who by means of secret favors has acquired a new state, that he must well consider the reasons which induced those to favor him who did so; and if it be not a natural affection towards him, but only discontent with their government, then he will only keep them friendly with great trouble and difficulty, for it will be impossible to satisfy them. And weighing well the reasons for this in those examples which can be taken from ancient and modern affairs, we shall find that it is easier for the prince to make friends of those men who were contented under the former government, and are therefore his enemies, than of those who, being discontented with it, were favorable to him and encouraged him to seize it.

6. It has been a custom with princes, in order to hold their states more securely, to build fortresses that may serve as a bridle and bit to those who might design to work against them, and as a place of refuge from a first attack. I praise this system because it has been made use of formerly. Notwithstanding that, Messer Niccolo Vitelli in our times has been seen to demolish two fortresses in Citta di Castello so that he might keep that state; Guido Ubaldo, Duke of Urbino, on returning to his dominion, whence he had been driven by Cesare Borgia, razed to the

foundations all the fortresses in that province, and considered that without them it would be more difficult to lose it; the Bentivogli returning to Bologna came to a similar decision. Fortresses, therefore, are useful or not according to circumstances; if they do you good in one way they injure you in another. And this question can be reasoned thus: the prince who has more to fear from the people than from foreigners ought to build fortresses, but he who has more to fear from foreigners than from the people ought to leave them alone. The castle of Milan, built by Francesco Sforza, has made, and will make, more trouble for the house of Sforza than any other disorder in the state. For this reason the best possible fortress is—not to be hated by the people, because, although you may hold the fortresses, yet they will not save you if the people hate you, for there will never be wanting foreigners to assist a people who have taken arms against you. It has not been seen in our times that such fortresses have been of use to any prince, unless to the Countess of Forli,* when the Count Girolamo, her consort, was killed; for by that means she was able to withstand the popular attack and wait for assistance from Milan, and thus recover her state; and the posture of affairs was

---

* Catherine Sforza, a daughter of Galeazzo Sforza and Lucrezia Landriani, born 1463, died 1509. It was to the Countess of Forli that Machiavelli was sent as envy on 1499. A letter from Fortunati to the countess announces the appointment: "I have been with the signori," wrote Fortunati, "to learn whom they would send and when. They tell me that Niccolo Machiavelli, a learned young Florentine noble, secretary to my Lords of the Ten, is to leave with me at once." Cf. "Catherine Sforza," by Count Pasolini, translated by P. Sylvester, 1898.

such at that time that the foreigners could not assist the people. But fortresses were of little value to her afterwards when Cesare Borgia attacked her, and when the people, her enemy, were allied with foreigners. Therefore, it would have been safer for her, both then and before, not to have been hated by the people than to have had the fortresses. All these things considered then, I shall praise him who builds fortresses as well as him who does not, and I shall blame whoever, trusting in them, cares little about being hated by the people.

STUDY GUIDE

Chapter XX

Leadership Trait #20
Strategic Thinking—
Ability to See the Big Picture and Think Ahead

In this chapter Machiavelli shares his opinion about a plethora of strategies that leaders utilized throughout his era in attempts to hold their states secure. He lists the strategies as:

- Disarming their subjects
- Keeping their subject towns distracted by factions
- Fostering enmities against themselves
- Laying themselves out to gain over those whom they distrusted in the beginning of their governments
- Building fortresses
- Overthrowing and destroying their subjects

Strategic Thinking—Ability to See the Big Picture and Think Ahead is the leadership trait outlined in this chapter. You could liken an effective leader to an outstanding chess player. Each is capable of planning for the present, while strategically thinking forward in time in anticipation of what might lie ahead. If strategic thinking is not a natural skill that you have, you can still develop the skills or find support staff that possesses them.

1. In the case of disarming your subjects, the author suggests that new princes arm their subjects, because in

doing so, create a new trust among those who were once mistrusted, along with a greater loyalty among their faithful soldiers. Applying this to your present day leadership initiatives,

2. In point #3, the author shares his opinions on whether it was best to hold states by factions (as was the case of Pistoia) or fortresses (as was the case with Pisa). He asserts that having factions (divided cities) would not create a strong front against the enemy, as the weakest party will crumble under siege. Do you believe this to be true regarding your leadership initiatives? Is it better to have all of your subordinates in one geographical location, or in a variety? Why?

3. In point #4, Machiavelli asserts that a wise leader will work to foster some animosity against him so that he could gain renown and respect by overcoming the challenge. Do you believe this is a wise strategy? Why or why not?

4. Have you ever fostered animosity in order to then gain respect by overcoming it? If so, what was the outcome?

5. Have you ever overcome animosity that you didn't craft? Were you respected more thereafter for doing so?

6. In point #5, the author asserts that princes, especially new ones experienced more fidelity and assistance by those who in the beginning were distrusted. Have you ever found this to be the case with you? Have there been individual who, in the beginning you did not trust, however later found them to be very supportive? If so, explain.

7. Some leaders may say that they have strong instincts about people and have never had a problem with distrusting a follower. Is this the case for you? Explain.

8. Machiavelli claims that it would be easier for a prince who has overthrown another to make friends with enemies who were loyal to the previous prince than with those who were already discontented with the previous leader. What are your thoughts on this theory?

9. Have you ever found this to be the case in your life? Explain.

10. In point #6, the author discusses the use of fortresses. He first suggests that they could be a place of refuge and a means to harness the attempts against the kingdom. Have you built emotional or other types of "fortresses" in your leadership initiatives? Explain.

11. Machiavelli also shares several cases in which the prince intentionally did not build or tore down existing fortress, claiming that they got in the way of their leadership. Have you ever been given a "fortress" or strong existing domain, and intentionally destroyed it? If so, explain. If not, are there ever situations in which you think this would be an effective strategy? Explain.

12. In the end, the author claims that while each case is unique, leaders who have more to fear from those within the culture over foreigners should build the fortress. In the end he claims that the best fortress is the love of one's followers. Do you believe this to be true? Cite at least one example where this is the case with a leader.

13. In relationship to your leadership desires and initiatives, how necessary do you believe your friendships to be in your life?

14. The leadership trait for this chapter is *strategic thinking—the ability to see the big picture and think ahead.* On a

scale from one to ten (one being "not at all" and ten being "a great deal"), rate how effective you are at strategic thinking:

1———2———3———4———5———6———7———8———9———10

15. In what ways are you a strategic thinker?

16. Provide examples in which you successfully applied strategic thinking to a situation.

17. Cite examples in which you unsuccessfully applied strategic thinking to a situation.

18. What have you done to hone your abilities as a strategic thinker?

19. What can you do to further develop these skills?

20. Do you have support staff or colleagues who are excellent strategic thinkers? If so, how might you better utilize their skills in your leadership initiatives?

21. If you don't have colleagues who are strategic thinkers, do you know of anyone who you could recruit? If not, what steps can you take to recruit one or two that do?

Chapter XXI

How a Prince Should Conduct Himself So as To Gain Renown

Nothing makes a prince so much esteemed as great enterprises and setting a fine example. We have in our time Ferdinand of Aragon, the present King of Spain.

He can almost be called a new prince, because he has risen, by fame and glory, from being an insignificant king to be the foremost king in Christendom; and if you will consider his deeds you will find them all great and some of them extraordinary. In the beginning of his reign he attacked Granada, and this enterprise was the foundation of his dominions. He did this quietly at first and without any fear of hindrance, for he held the minds of the barons of Castile occupied in thinking of the war and not anticipating any innovations; thus they did not perceive that by these means he was acquiring power and authority over them. He was able with the money of the Church and of the people to sustain his armies, and by that long war to lay the foundation for the military skill which has since distinguished him. Further, always using religion as a plea, so as to undertake greater schemes, he devoted himself with pious cruelty to driving out and clearing his kingdom of the Moors; nor could there be a more admirable example, nor one more rare. Under this same cloak he assailed Africa, he came down on Italy, he has finally attacked France; and thus his achievements and designs have always been great, and have kept the minds of his people in suspense and admiration and occupied with the issue of them. And his actions have arisen in such a way, one out of the other, that men have never been given time to work steadily against him.

Again, it much assists a prince to set unusual examples in internal affairs, similar to those which are related of Messer Bernabo da Milano, who, when he had the opportunity, by any one in civil life doing some extraordinary thing, either good or bad, would take some method of rewarding or punishing him, which would be much spoken about. And a prince ought, above all things, always endeavour in every action to gain for himself the reputation of being a great and remarkable man.

A prince is also respected when he is either a true friend or a downright enemy, that is to say, when, without any reservation, he declares himself in favor of one party against the other; which course will always be more advantageous than standing neutral; because if two of your powerful neighbors come to blows, they are of such a character that, if one of them conquers, you have either to fear him or not. In either case it will always be more advantageous for you to declare yourself and to make war strenuously; because, in the first case, if you do not declare yourself, you will invariably fall a prey to the conqueror, to the pleasure and satisfaction of him who has been conquered, and you will have no reasons to offer, nor anything to protect or to shelter you. Because he who conquers does not want doubtful friends who will not aid him in the time of trial; and he who loses will not harbor you because you did not willingly, sword in hand, court his fate.

Antiochus went into Greece, being sent for by the Aetolians to drive out the Romans. He sent envoys to the Achaeans, who were friends of the Romans, exhorting them to remain neutral; and on the other hand the Romans urged them to take up arms. This question came to be discussed in the council of the Achaeans, where the legate of Antiochus urged them to stand neutral. To this the Roman legate answered: "As for that which has been said, that it is better and more advantageous for your state not to interfere in our war, nothing can be more erroneous; because by not interfering you will be left, without favor or consideration, the guerdon of the conqueror." Thus it will always happen that he who is not your friend will demand your neutrality, whilst he who is your friend will entreat you to declare yourself with arms. And irresolute princes, to avoid present dangers, generally follow the neutral path, and are generally ruined. But when a prince declares himself gallantly in favor of one side, if the party with whom he allies himself conquers, although the victor may be powerful and may have him at his mercy, yet he is indebted to him, and there is established a bond of amity; and men are never so shameless as to become a monument of ingratitude by oppressing you. Victories after all are never so complete that the victor must not show some regard, especially to justice. But if he with whom you ally yourself loses, you may be sheltered by him, and whilst he is able he may aid you, and you become companions on a fortune that may rise again.

In the second case, when those who fight are of such a character that you have no anxiety as to who may conquer, so much the more is it greater prudence to be allied, because you assist at the destruction of one by the aid of another who, if he had been wise, would have saved him; and conquering, as it is impossible that he should not do with your assistance, he remains at your discretion. And here it is to be noted that a prince ought to take care never to make an alliance with one more powerful than himself for the purposes of attacking others, unless necessity compels him, as is said above; because if he conquers you are at his discretion, and princes ought to avoid as much as possible being at the discretion of any one. The Venetians joined with France against the Duke of Milan, and this alliance, which caused their ruin, could have been avoided. But when it cannot be avoided, as happened to the Florentines when the Pope and Spain sent armies to attack Lombardy, then in such a case, for the above reasons, the prince ought to favor one of the parties.

Never let any Government imagine that it can choose perfectly safe courses; rather let it expect to have to take very doubtful ones, because it is found in ordinary affairs that one never seeks to avoid one trouble without running into another; but prudence consists in knowing how to distinguish the character of troubles, and for choice to take the lesser evil.

A prince ought also to show himself a patron of ability, and to honor the proficient in every art. At the same time he should encourage his citizens to practice their callings peaceably, both in commerce and agriculture, and in every other following, so that the one should not be deterred from improving his possessions for fear lest they be taken away from him or another from opening up trade for fear of taxes; but the prince ought to offer rewards to whoever wishes to do these things and designs in any way to honor his city or state.

Further, he ought to entertain the people with festivals and spectacles at convenient seasons of the year; and as every city is divided into guilds or into societies,* he ought to hold such bodies in esteem, and associate with them sometimes, and show himself an example of courtesy and liberality; nevertheless, always maintaining the majesty of his rank, for this he must never consent to abate in anything.

---

* "Guilds or societies," "in arti o in tribu." "Arti" were craft or trade guilds, cf. Florio: "Arte . . . a whole company of any trade in any city or corporation town." The guilds of Florence are most admirably described by Mr. Edgcumbe Staley in his work on the subject (Methuen, 1906). Institutions of a somewhat similar character, called "artel," exist in Russia today, cf. Sir Mackenzie Wallace's "Russia," ed. 1905: "The sons . . . were always during the working season members of an artel. In some of the larger towns there are artels of a much more complex kind—permanent associations, possessing large capital, and pecuniarily responsible for the acts of the individual members." The word "artel," despite its apparent similarity, has, Mr. Aylmer Maude assures me, no connection with "ars" or "arte." Its root is that of the verb "rotisya," to bind oneself by an oath; and it is generally admitted to be only another form of "rota," which now signifies a "regimental company." In both words the underlying idea is that of a body of men united by an oath. "Tribu" were possibly gentile groups, united by common descent, and included individuals connected by marriage. Perhaps our words "sects" or "clans" would be most appropriate.

STUDY GUIDE

Chapter XXI

Leadership Trait #21
Stamina—
the Ability to Wade through Thick and Thin

Machiavelli opens this chapter emphasizing the importance of setting a good example, citing Ferdinand of Aragon, the King of Spain as a prime example. He then states that "nothing makes a prince so much esteemed as great enterprises and setting a fine example." He also states that Ferdinand "kept the minds of the people in suspense and admiration" as he conquered Africa, Italy and France. Thus, Ferdinand possessed a multitude of admirable traits as a leader, all of which served as examples of powerful leadership to those who followed him. He also credited Ferdinand for taking a strong stance, when he states, "A prince is also respected when he is either a true friend or a downright enemy, that is to say, when, without any reservation, he declares himself in favor of one party against the other; which course will always be more advantageous than standing neutral. He ends the chapter asserting that a prince should "show himself a patron of ability, and honor the proficient in every art." He continues by stating, "he should encourage his citizens to practice their callings peaceably, so as not to deter them from improving their possessions.

The leadership trait associated with this chapter is *loyalty—the ability to stand by others through thick and thin.* While loyalty is a trait that is valued by all, it is of particular importance when you are in pursuit of a leadership role. Loyal leaders most often have loyal subjects, for you draw to yourself that which you are. Loyal followers are of utmost importance as you pursue your leadership goals. Loyalty and trust are the foundation upon which solid relationships are built.

1. List at least three people who you believe are exemplary models of leadership.

2. For each of the above leaders, list the traits they possess that you believe makes them exceptional models of leadership.

3. What are the three traits you most need to focus on in order to become an outstanding leader?

4. Ferdinand is described as "using religion as a pea, so as to undertake greater schemes. He devoted himself with "pious cruelty". What do you think this means?

5. Do you believe this to be a noble trait that you would want to follow as a leader?

6. Ferdinand "kept the minds of the people in suspense and admiration" as he conquered Africa, Italy and France. How do you create "suspense and admiration" as a leader?

7. Machiavelli cites Messer Bernabo da Milano as an example of a leader who always made it a point to reward or punish his internal affairs members for extraordinary acts. How do you believe this behavior gained him respect as a leader?

8. Do you reward or punish your subordinates? If so, how?

9. What initiatives could you start that would further reward or punish those who report to you?

10. According to the author "a prince is also respected when he is either a true friend or a downright enemy." He claims that whatever the circumstances may be, standing in a neutral position is not effective. What are your thoughts on this viewpoint?

11. Are you strong in your convictions, or do you tend to remain more neutral? On a scale from one to ten (one being "neutral" and ten being "very firm in my convictions"), rate your position on neutrality versus firmness:

1——2——3——4——5——6——7——8——9——10

12. What decisions or initiatives could you take immediately to become firmer in your stance?

13. The leadership trait associated with this chapter is *loyalty—the ability to stand by others through thick and thin.* Machiavelli states "he who conquers does not want doubtful friends who will not aid him in the time of trial." On a scale from one to ten (one being "not at all" and ten being "very much"), rate how loyal a friend you believe yourself to be:

14. On a scale from one to ten (one being "not at all" and ten being "very much"), rate how loyal an employee or colleague you believe yourself to be:

1——2——3——4——5——6——7——8——9——10

15. Machiavelli states, "he who is not your friend will demand your neutrality, whilst he who is your fiend will entreat you to declare yourself with arms." On a scale from one to ten (one being "not at all" and ten being "a great deal"), rate how loyal your friend are towards you:

1——2——3——4——5——6——7——8——9——10

16. Loyalty among staff and co-workers is also important. On a scale from one to ten (one being "not at all" and ten being "a great deal"), rate how loyal your staff and co-workers are towards you:

1——2——3——4——5——6——7——8——9——10

17. Machiavelli warns that "a prince ought to take care never to make an alliance with one more powerful than himself for the purposes of attacking others…because if he conquers you are at his discretion." Do you agree? Why or why not?

18. Have you ever allied yourself with one more powerful than you? What was the outcome?

19. The author also warns about false security, asserting that knowing the character of your challenges is key. Do you ever believe yourself or your subordinates to have a false sense of security? Explain.

20. According to Machiavelli, a prince should "show himself a patron of ability, and honor the proficient in every art". He continues by stating, "he should encourage his citizens to practice their callings peaceably, so as not to deter them from improving their possessions. Do you encourage your colleagues and subordinates to do their best, and gain their own success?

21. On a scale from one to ten (one being "not at all" and ten being "a great deal"), rate how encouraging you are towards your teams' personal endeavors:

1——2——3——4——5——6——7——8——9——10

22. How do you currently honor the successes of other who work with or for you?

23. List three more creative ways that you could start to honor the successes of others.

24. Being jealous of others is natural; however it can get in the way of your success if you respond to it in a negative way. Do you ever struggle with jealousy when others are successful?

25. Have you ever responded negatively? If so, how?

26. Sometimes making a concerted effort to catch others doing things right, and openly praising them for it can make both you and them feel better. What do you do to work through the jealousy?

27. The author asserts that effective princes hold festivals and spectacles for those whom they oversee. Do you take time to honor your support staff or others in such a way? List such events that you hold.

28. What additional events could you hold to create honor, fun and appreciation towards others? List them and then set dates to implement them within the next year.

29. According to Machiavelli, effective princes also hold guilds and societies in esteem. Do you belong to any guilds or societies? If so, list them. If not, are there any that you are currently interested in. Investigate and join at least one guild or society that you find interesting.

30. Do you support guilds or societies? Perhaps you volunteer at their events, or donate your time or money towards their cause. Describe how you lend support to them.

31. What further initiatives could you take towards supporting them?

32. Finally, Machiavelli ends the chapter asserting that the wise leader "always maintains the majesty of his rank, for this he must never consent to abate in anything". Do you believe you hold true to your position at all times? Explain.

Chapter XXII

Concerning the Secretaries of Princes

The choice of servants is of no little importance to a prince, and they are good or not according to the discrimination of the prince. And the first opinion which one forms of a prince, and of his understanding, is by observing the men he has around him; and when they are capable and faithful he may always be considered wise, because he has known how to recognize the capable and to keep them faithful. But when they are otherwise one cannot form a good opinion of him, for the prime error which he made was in choosing them.

There were none who knew Messer Antonio da Venafro as the servant of Pandolfo Petrucci, Prince of Siena, who would not consider Pandolfo to be a very clever man in having Venafro for his servant. Because there are three classes of intellects: one which comprehends by itself; another which appreciates what others comprehended; and a third which neither comprehends by itself nor by the showing of others; the first is the most excellent, the second is good, the third is useless. Therefore, it follows necessarily that, if Pandolfo was not in the first rank, he was in the second, for whenever one has judgment to know good and bad when it is said and done, although he himself may not have the initiative, yet he can recognize the good and the bad in his servant, and the one he can praise and the other correct; thus the servant cannot hope to deceive him, and is kept honest. But to enable a prince to form an opinion of his servant there is one test which never fails; when you see the servant thinking more of his own interests than of yours, and seeking inwardly his own profit in everything, such a man will never make a good servant, nor will you ever be able to trust him; because he who has the state of another in his hands ought never to think of himself, but always of his prince, and never pay any attention to matters in which the prince is not concerned.

On the other hand, to keep his servant honest the prince ought to study him, honoring him, enriching him, doing him kindnesses, sharing with him the honors and cares; and at the same time let him see that he cannot stand alone, so that many honors may not make him desire more, many riches make him wish for more, and that many cares may make him dread chances. When, therefore, servants, and princes towards servants, are thus disposed, they can trust each other, but when it is otherwise, the end will always be disastrous for either one or the other.

Chapter XXII

Leadership Trait #22
Economy—Ability to Achieve Much with Very Little

Machiavelli opens this chapter asserting that princes should use discrimination when choosing servants, for they are a reflection of his abilities to choose staff wisely. He describes three classes of intellects: 1) Those who comprehend of their own accord (which he considers good), 2) Those who appreciate what others comprehend (which he considers excellent), and 3) Those who comprehend nothing nor appreciate it in others (which he considers useless). He suggests that a good prince would be kept honest in possessing such traits. He said that the test of a good servant is to note if he or she becomes more interested in his or her own self-interests over caring for you. He ends the chapter encouraging being kind, sharing, enriching and honoring good servants, while at the same time letting them see that they cannot stand alone—they need you.

Economy—the ability to achieve much with very little is the leadership trait affiliated with this chapter. In order to be economical, one has to be both committed and creative. Economical leaders are respected among their peers and followers, for they waste nothing and are able to create the remarkable with very little. While this trait is not innate in everyone, you can take specific steps towards strategizing economically as you pursue your leadership goals.

1. Do you personally choose those that work for you, or does someone else choose on your behalf? On a scale from one to ten (one being "poor"and ten being "excellent"), rate how effective you are at reading people:

1——2——3——4——5——6——7——8——9——10

2. On a scale from one to ten (one being "poor" and ten being"excellent"), rate how effective those that work for you are:

1——2——3——4——5——6——7——8——9——10

3. Machiavelli describes three classes of intellects: 1) Those who comprehend of their own accord (which he considers good) 2) Those who appreciate what others comprehend (which he considers excellent) and 3) Those who comprehend nothing nor appreciate it in others (which he considers useless). Which of the three do you believe best describes you? Why?

4. On a scale from one to ten (one being "poor" and ten being"excellent"), rate how effective you are at appreciating the intellect of others:

1——2——3——4——5——6——7——8——9——10

5. Why do you think Machiavelli asserts that possessing the traits in 1) and 2) will keep a leader honest?

6. Do you believe that those who work for you should always put your best interest over theirs? Explain.

7. Do you believe that expecting those who work for you to be more interested in your best interest than their own to be realistic?

8. Write a list of what your expectations are for those who work for you.

9. What rules must they follow? At what point do you draw the line on their self-interested behaviors?

10. Write a list of the things that you do to be kind to your subordinates.

11. List the things that you share with your subordinates.

12. Write a list of the opportunities you provide your subordinates that enrich their lives.

13. What do you do to honor your subordinates?

14. List the things that you can do to further show kindness, to share, enrich and honor those who work for you?

15. The leadership trait listed with this chapter is *economy—the ability to achieve much with very little*. On a scale from one to ten (one being "poor" and ten being "excellent"), rate how effective you are at economizing:

1——2——3——4——5——6——7——8——9——10

16. What do you do to effectively economize? Write a list of the ways in which you do.

17. What steps can you take to better economize in your personal life?

18. What steps can you take to better economize in your professional life?

19. What benefits will come to you both in your personal and professional life once you further economize?

Chapter XXIII

How Flatterers Should Be Avoided

I do not wish to leave out an important branch of this subject, for it is a danger from which princes are with difficulty preserved, unless they are very careful and discriminating. It is that of flatterers, of whom courts are full, because men are so self-complacent in their own affairs, and in a way so deceived in them, that they are preserved with difficulty from this pest, and if they wish to defend themselves they run the danger of falling into contempt. Because there is no other way of guarding oneself from flatterers except letting men understand that to tell you the truth does not offend you; but when everyone may tell you the truth, respect for you abates.

Therefore a wise prince ought to hold a third course by choosing the wise men in his state, and giving to them only the liberty of speaking the truth to him, and then only of those things of which he inquires, and of none others; but he ought to question them upon everything, and listen to their opinions, and afterwards form his own conclusions. With these councilors, separately and collectively, he ought to carry himself in such a way that each of them should know that, the more freely he shall speak, the more he shall be preferred; outside of these, he should listen to no one, pursue the thing resolved on, and be steadfast in his resolutions. He who does otherwise is either overthrown by flatterers, or is so often changed by varying opinions that he falls into contempt.

I wish on this subject to adduce a modern example. Fra Luca, the man of affairs to Maximilian,* the present emperor, speaking of his majesty, said: He consulted with no one, yet never got his own way in anything. This arose because of his following a practice the opposite to the above; for the emperor is a secretive man—he does not communicate his designs to any one, nor does he receive opinions on them. But as in carrying them into effect they become revealed and known, they are at once obstructed by those men whom he has around him, and he, being pliant, is diverted from them. Hence it follows that those things he does one day he undoes the next, and no one ever understands what he wishes or intends to do, and no one can rely on his resolutions.

A prince, therefore, ought always to take counsel, but only when he wishes and not when others wish; he ought rather to discourage everyone from offering advice unless he asks it; but, however, he ought to be a constant inquirer, and afterwards a patient listener concerning the things of which he inquired; also, on learning that any

---

* Maximilian I, born in 1459, died 1519, Emperor of the Holy Roman Empire. He married, first, Mary, daughter of Charles the Bold; after her death, Bianca Sforza; and thus became involved in Italian politics.

one, on any consideration, has not told him the truth, he should let his anger be felt.

And if there are some who think that a prince who conveys an impression of his wisdom is not so through his own ability, but through the good advisers that he has around him, beyond doubt they are deceived, because this is an axiom which never fails: that a prince who is not wise himself will never take good advice, unless by chance he has yielded his affairs entirely to one person who happens to be a very prudent man. In this case indeed he may be well governed, but it would not be for long, because such a governor would in a short time take away his state from him.

But if a prince who is not inexperienced should take counsel from more than one he will never get united counsels, nor will he know how to unite them. Each of the counsellors will think of his own interests, and the prince will not know how to control them or to see through them. And they are not to found otherwise, because men will always prove untrue to you unless they are kept honest by constraint. Therefore it must be inferred that good counsels, whencesoever they come, are born of the wisdom of the prince and not the wisdom of the prince from good counsels.

Chapter XXIII

Leadership Trait #23
Decisiveness—
Ability to Make Immediate Decisions

Machiavelli warns against the danger of flatterers in this chapter. He suggests that good princes encourage the truth from their followers and choose wise councilors in his state with whom he avidly listens and inquires. While he should remain confident and steadfast in his decisions, he should inform them that the more freely they speak, the more he or she will favor them. He cites Fra Luca as an example of a leader taking initiative and then changing it because those around him obstructed it. In this case Machiavelli asserted that no one could therefore rely on his resolutions. He suggests that princes should be constant inquirers and good listeners, however, only taking advice if they specifically ask for it. In the end he asserts that good princes are not so because they have good counsel, but they have good counsel because they are good princes.

The leadership trait associated with this chapter is *decisiveness—the ability to make immediate decisions.* One of the most impressive traits of a successful leader is his or her ability to be laser sharp and decisive when it comes to making decisions. There is little time for weighing the odds, for decisive leaders are able to make decisions very quickly and at a moment's notice. To gain the respect of their followers, they never question their choices and proceed with confidence and conviction.

1. Make a list of those you believe to be flatterers in your life.

2. How do you distinguish the difference between flatterers and those who legitimately honor and respect you?

3. Is there anyone in your life that you flatter? Who and why?

4. Like Machiavelli, do you believe that flatterers are a danger? Why or why not?

5. Do you have a "council" of wise colleagues in whom you trust and seek advice?

6. Make a list of the individuals with whom you seek advice.

7. Is there anyone not among your council that you would like to add?

8. Are there any areas of your leadership endeavors that require additional wisdom and guidance? If so, explain.

9. Are there additional individual(s) that you would like to include among your circle of trusted council? Write a list and take the initiative to start a conversation with those with whom you are interested.

10. Do you encourage directness and honesty from those with whom you trust? How might you further do so?

11. Do you ever meet with your wise colleagues in a formal setting to receive their input? Why or why not?

12. Are you a constant inquirer? On a scale from one to ten (one being "poor" and ten being "excellent"), rate how effective an inquirer you are:

1——2——3——4——5——6——7——8——9——10

13. What exercises could you do to improve upon your ability to research or inquire?

14. Schedule time to practice inquiry, even if only 5 minutes each week. Journal about your progress.

15. Take some time to journal about the times that you are being an effective leader. Often when you focus your attention on a positive practice, the positive experiences begin to grow.

16. The leadership trait referenced with this chapter is *deci-siveness—the ability to make immediate decisions*. While you may be an excellent inquirer and listener, if you are not able to make immediate decisions, these traits are useless. On a scale from one to ten (one being "poor"and ten being "excellent"), rate how effective you are at being decisive:

1———2———3———4———5———6———7———8———9———10

17. What prevents you from making quick decisions?

18. During what kind of circumstances do you find it easy to make decisions?

19. When you are indecisive, what are the negative ramifications of your inaction

20. When you are decisive, do you experience negative ramifications? If so, what?

21. Do you find that the outcome is often successful when you trust your hunches and make quick decisions? Explain.

22. What action steps can you take towards becoming more confident in decision-making?

23. Create an action plan and began to further work on your decision-making skills. Write about your experience when doing so.

Chapter XXIV

Why the Princes of Italy
Have Lost Their States

The previous suggestions, carefully observed, will enable a new prince to appear well established, and render him at once more secure and fixed in the state than if he had been long seated there. For the actions of a new prince are more narrowly observed than those of an hereditary one, and when they are seen to be able they gain more men and bind far tighter than ancient blood; because men are attracted more by the present than by the past, and when they find the present good they enjoy it and seek no further; they will also make the utmost defense of a prince if he fails them not in other things. Thus it will be a double glory for him to have established a new principality, and adorned and strengthened it with good laws, good arms, good allies, and with a good example; so will it be a double disgrace to him who, born a prince, shall lose his state by want of wisdom.

And if those seigniors are considered who have lost their states in Italy in our times, such as the King of

Naples, the Duke of Milan, and others, there will be found in them, firstly, one common defect in regard to arms from the causes which have been discussed at length; in the next place, some one of them will be seen, either to have had the people hostile, or if he has had the people friendly, he has not known how to secure the nobles. In the absence of these defects states that have power enough to keep an army in the field cannot be lost.

Philip of Macedon, not the father of Alexander the Great, but he who was conquered by Titus Quintius, had not much territory compared to the greatness of the Romans and of Greece who attacked him, yet being a warlike man who knew how to attract the people and secure the nobles, he sustained the war against his enemies for many years, and if in the end he lost the dominion of some cities, nevertheless he retained the kingdom.

Therefore, do not let our princes accuse fortune for the loss of their principalities after so many years' possession, but rather their own sloth, because in quiet times they never thought there could be a change (it is a common defect in man not to make any provision in the calm against the tempest), and when afterwards the bad times came they thought of flight and not of defending themselves, and they hoped that the people, disgusted with the insolence of the conquerors, would recall them. This course, when others fail, may be good, but it is very bad to have neglected all other expedients for that, since you would never wish to fall because you trusted to be able to find someone later on to restore you. This again either does not happen, or, if it does, it will not be for your security, because that deliverance is of no avail which does not depend upon yourself; those only are reliable, certain, and durable that depend on yourself and your valor.

STUDY GUIDE

Chapter XXIV

Leadership Trait #24
Vision—Ability to See Possibilities

In this chapter Machiavelli shares insights on why he believed some of Italy's princes lost their states. He opens by stating that new princes should do well if they follow the guidelines he set out in this treatise. He claims that when a new prince fairs well, he gains stronger bonds with more men than those who have inherited their position. Followers will defend a good leader, especially one who establishes a new principality and strengthens it with good laws, good arms, good allies, and with a good example. In the case of princes who are born into a state, they can be doubly disgraced without such wisdom. Citing the King of Naples and the Duke of Milan, Machiavelli asserts that, among other things, they did not follow the guidelines outlined and/or created hostile or insecure environments. He then cites Philip of Macedon as an example of a successful leader. While he did not have much territory, he was able to secure the nobles and kept the enemies at bay for great lengths of time. To end this chapter, he emphasizes that princes have not lost their kingdoms through misfortune, but through laziness and being ill-prepared.

Vision—the ability to see possibilities is this chapter's leadership trait. Not only are effective leaders visionaries, but they are also able to create visions in the hearts and minds of their followers. First you must have a vision as a leader. Without the ability to see, hear, smell, touch and feel what is possible, you cannot manifest your greatest dreams into your life. Visionaries have little time for negative thinking, and are able to forge ahead towards their vision, whatever the climate may be.

1. Machiavelli opens this chapter by stating that new princes would do well if they studied and practiced the behaviors outlined in this treatise. Do you believe this to be so? Do you think this treatise is comprehensive and useful for new leaders? Why or why not?

2. What do you believe is lacking in Machiavelli's advice?

3. What are the most poignant lessons the author has taught you thus far? Explain.

4. Do you believe that poor leadership is often due to laziness? Explain.

5. What do you see as the prime reasons why leaders tend to fail?

6. Do you believe that many fail because of being ill-prepared?

7. Have you ever failed an endeavor because you do not properly prepare? Explain.

8. Do you have assistance in preparing for your leadership initiatives?

9. Very often when getting a new endeavor started, we spend too much time doing the mundane, groundwork ourselves, leaving little time to focus on the important things. Is this the case with you?

10. What could you do to provide yourself more time to focus on the important items, over that which is necessary but not a good use of your skills and time?

11. On a scale from one to ten (one being "not at all" and ten being "a great deal"), rate how lazy you believe yourself to be:

12. In what areas do you find yourself to be lazy?

13. Are the areas in which you find yourself lazy, areas that you are not particularly passionate about?

14. Write a list of the things that you do that you are not passionate about.

15. Go through the list you created, could you find someone else to accomplish those tasks on your behalf? If so, take some time to seek someone out to do that work for you. Write about your experience and any blocks, victories or overall changes that you note.

16. *Vision—the ability to see possibilities* is the leadership trait associated with this chapter. On a scale from one to ten (one being "not at all"and ten being "a great deal"), rate how much vision you possess:

17. How do you define "vision" as it pertains to your life and more specifically, your leadership initiatives?

18. Do you sometimes have tunnel vision when focusing on your goals and initiatives? If so, do you think having this kind of vision impedes up or encourages your success? Explain.

19. Taking time each day to envision your goals, seeing them successfully manifest can greatly impact your success. Do you take time each day to envision the ideal outcome of your goals?

20. Feeling the success of the goals as you envision them is key to your success. The more you see, hear, smell and feel them in the present moment, the stronger you attract them to you. Are you able to use multiple senses when envisioning the manifestation of your goals in your life? Explain.

21. The mind does not discern the difference between "experiencing" something and "envisioning" it. Thus, you should spend at least a couple of minutes each day envisioning your success. Doing so can assist in manifesting them in your life. What other steps can you take towards improving your vision as you journey towards manifesting your leadership goals?

Chapter XXV

What Fortune Can Effect in Human Affairs and How to Withstand Her

I t is not unknown to me how many men have had, and still have, the opinion that the affairs of the world are in such wise governed by fortune and by God that men with their wisdom cannot direct them and that no one can even help them; and because of this they would have us believe that it is not necessary to labour much in affairs, but to let chance govern them. This opinion has been more credited in our times because of the great changes in affairs which have been seen, and may still be seen, every day, beyond all human conjecture. Sometimes pondering over this, I am in some degree inclined to their opinion. Nevertheless, not to extinguish our free will, I hold it to be true that Fortune is the arbiter of one-half of our actions,* but that she still leaves us to direct the other half, or perhaps a little less.

---

* Frederick the Great was accustomed to say: "The older one gets the more convinced one becomes that his Majesty King Chance does three-quarters of the business of this miserable universe." Sorel's "Eastern Question."

I compare her to one of those raging rivers, which when in flood overflows the plains, sweeping away trees and buildings, bearing away the soil from place to place; everything flies before it, all yield to its violence, without being able in any way to withstand it; and yet, though its nature be such, it does not follow therefore that men, when the weather becomes fair, shall not make provision, both with defenses and barriers, in such a manner that, rising again, the waters may pass away by canal, and their force be neither so unrestrained nor so dangerous. So it happens with fortune, who shows her power where valor has not prepared to resist her, and thither she turns her forces where she knows that barriers and defenses have not been raised to constrain her.

And if you will consider Italy, which is the seat of these changes, and which has given to them their impulse, you will see it to be an open country without barriers and without any defense. For if it had been defended by proper valor, as are Germany, Spain, and France, either this invasion would not have made the great changes it has made or it would not have come at all. And this I consider enough to say concerning resistance to fortune in general.

But confining myself more to the particular, I say that a prince may be seen happy to-day and ruined to-morrow without having shown any change of disposition or character. This, I believe, arises firstly from causes that have already been discussed at length, namely, that the prince who relies entirely on fortune is lost when it changes. I believe also that he will be successful who directs his actions according to the spirit of the times, and that he whose actions do not accord with the times will not be successful. Because men are seen, in affairs that lead to the end which every man has before him, namely, glory and riches, to get there by various methods; one with caution, another with haste; one by force, another by skill; one by patience, another by its opposite; and each one succeeds in reaching the goal by a different method. One can also see of two cautious men the one attain his end, the other fail; and similarly, two men by different observances are equally successful, the one being cautious, the other impetuous; all this arises from nothing else than whether or not they conform in their methods to the spirit of the times. This follows from what I have said, that two men working differently bring about the same effect, and of two working similarly, one attains his object and the other does not.

Changes in estate also issue from this, for if, to one who governs himself with caution and patience, times and affairs converge in such a way that his administration is successful, his fortune is made; but if times and affairs change, he is ruined if he does not change his course of action. But a man is not often found sufficiently circumspect to know how to accommodate himself to the change, both because he cannot deviate from what nature inclines him to do, and also because, having always prospered by acting in one way, he cannot be persuaded that it is well to leave it; and, therefore, the cautious man, when it is time to turn adventurous, does not know how to do it, hence he is ruined; but had he changed his conduct with the times fortune would not have changed.

Pope Julius the Second went to work impetuously in all his affairs, and found the times and circumstances conform so well to that line of action that he always met with success. Consider his first enterprise against Bologna, Messer Giovanni Bentivogli being still alive. The Venetians were not agreeable to it, nor was the King of Spain, and he had the enterprise still under discussion with the King of France; nevertheless he personally entered upon the expedition with his accustomed boldness and energy, a move which made Spain and the Venetians stand irresolute and passive, the latter from fear, the former from desire to recover the kingdom of Naples; on the other hand, he drew after him the King of France, because that king, having observed the movement, and desiring to make the Pope his friend so as to humble the Venetians, found it impossible to refuse him. Therefore Julius with his impetuous action accomplished what no other pontiff with simple human wisdom could have done; for if he had waited in Rome until he could get away, with his plans arranged and everything fixed, as any other pontiff would have done, he would never have succeeded. Because the King of France would have made a thousand excuses, and the others would have raised a thousand fears.

I will leave his other actions alone, as they were all alike, and they all succeeded, for the shortness of his life did not let him experience the contrary; but if circumstances had arisen which required him to go cautiously, his ruin would have followed, because he would never have deviated from those ways to which nature inclined him.

I conclude, therefore that, fortune being changeful and mankind steadfast in their ways, so long as the two are in agreement men are successful, but unsuccessful when they fall out. For my part I consider that it is better to be adventurous than cautious, because fortune is a woman, and if you wish to keep her under it is necessary to beat and ill-use her; and it is seen that she allows herself to be mastered by the adventurous rather than by those who go to work more coldly. She is, therefore, always, woman-like, a lover of young men, because they are less cautious, more violent, and with more audacity command her.

STUDY GUIDE

Chapter XXV

Leadership Trait #25
Operational—Ability to See the Big Picture

In this chapter Machiavelli shares insights on how to overcome the odds, especially when the economy turns. He opens with an observation around the opinions of life is controlled by luck or God, as opposed to the theory that we have control. While he leaves the argument open, he stresses that if Fortune is the arbiter of half of our actions, we are still responsible for the other half. He discusses how you can use such downturns so that they work in your favor. Likening luck to the unpredictability of nature, he suggests that preparation and right action are still key, despite that which we have no control over. He cites Italy as an example of a country that was not prepared or defended, and because of this, experienced great turmoil. He then goes on to state that with variances of style and strategies, a leader is best to be true to the present, not relying on the initiatives of past victors. One has to be malleable and move with the times, ready to re-strategize should the need arise. He then cites Pope Julius the Second as a prime example of a leader who worked "impetuously" in all his affairs, and conformed to the necessary actions at the right times, thus achieving great success. Machiavelli uses a crude parallel as he ends the chapter—one that many would consider offensive. He encourages adventure over caution, likening Fortune to a woman, stating *"Fortune is a woman, and if you wish to keep her under it is necessary to beat and ill-use her; and it is seen that she allows herself to be mastered by the adventurous rather than by those who go to work more coldly. She is, therefore, always, woman-like, a lover of young men, because they are less cautious, more violent, and with more audacity command her."*

The leadership trait outlined in this chapter is the ability to be *operational—to see the big picture.* Operational thinkers display real leadership in their ability to see so far beyond that which is simply in front of them. They are able to see each cog in the wheel of their success plan and in doing so can ensure that all of the parts are moving in tandem. With effective coaching and structural practices in place, you can take your vision far beyond what you originally thought was imaginable.

1. Machiavelli opens this chapter debating whether God or good fortune exist. Do you believe in God? Explain.

2. Do you believe in luck? Explain.

3. Do you believe that luck or fortune have played a part in your successes and failures in life? Explain.

4. Do you believe you make your own luck? Explain.

5. Machiavelli encourages leaders to be malleable and willing to roll with the times. In what situations have you changed your strategies or initiatives because of shifted circumstances? Explain.

6. Have you ever had situations where you did not shift initiatives, only to find your opportunity lost because of your lack of flexibility? Explain.

7. Write a list of potential situations would shift your current leadership initiatives.

8. For each item on the list, write your strategic response to the shift.

9. Preparation and immediate action are key—just like the analogy Machiavelli used with the unpredictability of nature. Write a list of unpredictable situations that arose in your life.

10. Were you prepared and able to take immediate action when the unexpected arose for the situations listed above? Explain.

11. Did preparation help? Why or why not?

12. Are there times when you found that your preparation negatively affected the outcome of an unexpected situation? Explain.

13. Do you have emergency funds set aside just in case you met an unexpected downturn? Why or why not?

14. Do you believe you have enough money put away to support you should upset arise in your life? If not, how much more do you think you would need to feel secure?

15. What action steps can you take towards having the necessary emergency funds? Write out a plan, and commit to following it.

16. Do you find Machiavelli's final analogy between Fortune and women offensive? Why or why not? Explain.

17. The leadership trait assigned to this chapter is the possession of *an operational mindset—the ability to see the big picture.* On a scale from one to ten (one being "not at all" and ten being "a great deal"), rate how effective you are at seeing the big picture:

1——2——3——4——5——6——7——8——9——10

18. If you have an operational mindset, you are able to see the big picture— how all the cogs work together to make things run smoothly. On a scale from one to ten (one being "not at all" and ten being "a great deal"), rate how operationally effective your leadership initiatives are:

1——2——3——4——5——6——7——8——9——10

19. Are there any areas of your business or leadership strategy that are not fully functional? List them.

20. What action steps can you take to improve upon these areas?

21. If you are not as effective as you would like to be at seeing the big picture, do you have individuals working with you who have operational mindsets? If not, make a point of finding someone who does, and add him or her to your team.

22. In juxtaposition with the operational mind is the detail-oriented mindset. On a scale from one to ten (one being "not at all" and ten being "a great deal"), rate how effective you are with details:

1——2——3——4——5——6——7——8——9——10

23. Do you have individuals who are detailed-oriented that could assist you? If not, be sure to find someone who could.

Chapter XXVI

An Exhortation to Liberate Italy from the Barbarians

Having carefully considered the subject of the above discourses, and wondering within myself whether the present times were propitious to a new prince, and whether there were elements that would give an opportunity to a wise and virtuous one to introduce a new order of things which would do honor to him and good to the people of this country, it appears to me that so many things concur to favor a new prince that I never knew a time more fit than the present.

And if, as I said, it was necessary that the people of Israel should be captive so as to make manifest the ability of Moses; that the Persians should be oppressed by the Medes so as to discover the greatness of the soul of Cyrus; and that the Athenians should be dispersed to illustrate the capabilities of Theseus: then at the present time, in order to discover the virtue of an Italian spirit, it was necessary that Italy should be reduced to the extremity that she is now in, that she should be more enslaved than the Hebrews, more oppressed than the Persians, more scattered than the Athenians; without head, without order, beaten, despoiled, torn, overrun; and to have endured every kind of desolation.

Although lately some spark may have been shown by one, which made us think he was ordained by God for our redemption, nevertheless it was afterwards seen, in the height of his career, that fortune rejected him; so that Italy, left as without life, waits for him who shall yet heal her wounds and put an end to the ravaging and plundering of Lombardy, to the swindling and taxing of the kingdom and of Tuscany, and cleanse those sores that for long have festered. It is seen how she entreats God to send someone who shall deliver her from these wrongs and barbarous insolencies. It is seen also that she is ready and willing to follow a banner if only someone will raise it.

Nor is there to be seen at present one in whom she can place more hope than in your illustrious house,* with its valor and fortune, favored by God and by the Church of which it is now the chief, and which could be made the head of this redemption. This will not be difficult if you will recall to yourself the actions and lives of the men I have named. And although they were great and wonderful men, yet they were men, and each one of them had no more opportunity than the present offers, for their enterprises were neither more just nor easier than this, nor was God more their friend than He is yours.

---

* Giuliano de Medici. He had just been created a cardinal by Leo X. In 1523 Giuliano was elected Pope, and took the title of Clement VII.

With us there is great justice, because that war is just which is necessary, and arms are hallowed when there is no other hope but in them. Here there is the greatest willingness, and where the willingness is great the difficulties cannot be great if you will only follow those men to whom I have directed your attention. Further than this, how extraordinarily the ways of God have been manifested beyond example: the sea is divided, a cloud has led the way, the rock has poured forth water, it has rained manna, everything has contributed to your greatness; you ought to do the rest. God is not willing to do everything, and thus take away our free will and that share of glory which belongs to us.

And it is not to be wondered at if none of the above-named Italians have been able to accomplish all that is expected from your illustrious house; and if in so many revolutions in Italy, and in so many campaigns, it has always appeared as if military virtue were exhausted, this has happened because the old order of things was not good, and none of us have known how to find a new one. And nothing honors a man more than to establish new laws and new ordinances when he himself was newly risen. Such things when they are well founded and dignified will make him revered and admired, and in Italy there are not wanting opportunities to bring such into use in every form.

Here there is great valor in the limbs whilst it fails in the head. Look attentively at the duels and the hand-to-hand combats, how superior the Italians are in strength, dexterity, and subtlety. But when it comes to armies they do not bear comparison, and this springs entirely from the insufficiency of the leaders, since those who are capable are not obedient, and each one seems to himself to know, there having never been any one so distinguished above the rest, either by valor or fortune, that others would yield to him. Hence it is that for so long a time, and during so much fighting in the past twenty years, whenever there has been an army wholly Italian, it has always given a poor account of itself; the first witness to this is Il Taro, afterwards Allesandria, Capua, Genoa, Vaila, Bologna, Mestri.*

If, therefore, your illustrious house wishes to follow these remarkable men who have redeemed their country, it is necessary before all things, as a true foundation for every enterprise, to be provided with your own forces, because there can be no more faithful, truer, or better soldiers. And although singly they are good, altogether they will be much better when they find themselves commanded by their prince, honored by him, and maintained at his expense. Therefore it is necessary to be prepared with such arms, so that you can be defended against foreigners by Italian valor.

And although Swiss and Spanish infantry may be considered very formidable, nevertheless there is a defect in both, by reason of which a third order would not only be able to oppose them, but might be relied upon to overthrow them. For the Spaniards cannot resist cavalry, and the Switzers are afraid of infantry whenever they

---

* The battles of Il Taro, 1495; Alessandria, 1499; Capua, 1501; Genoa, 1507; Vaila, 1509; Bologna, 1511; Mestri, 1513.

encounter them in close combat. Owing to this, as has been and may again be seen, the Spaniards are unable to resist French cavalry, and the Switzers are overthrown by Spanish infantry. And although a complete proof of this latter cannot be shown, nevertheless there was some evidence of it at the battle of Ravenna, when the Spanish infantry were confronted by German battalions, who follow the same tactics as the Swiss; when the Spaniards, by agility of body and with the aid of their shields, got in under the pikes of the Germans and stood out of danger, able to attack, while the Germans stood helpless, and, if the cavalry had not dashed up, all would have been over with them. It is possible, therefore, knowing the defects of both these infantries, to invent a new one, which will resist cavalry and not be afraid of infantry; this need not create a new order of arms, but a variation upon the old. And these are the kind of improvements which confer reputation and power upon a new prince.

This opportunity, therefore, ought not to be allowed to pass for letting Italy at last see her liberator appear. Nor can one express the love with which he would be received in all those provinces which have suffered so much from these foreign scourings, with what thirst for revenge, with what stubborn faith, with what devotion, with what tears. What door would be closed to him? Who would refuse obedience to him? What envy would hinder him? What Italian would refuse him homage? To all of us this barbarous dominion stinks. Let, therefore, your illustrious house take up this charge with that courage and hope with which all just enterprises are undertaken, so that under its standard our native country may be ennobled, and under its auspices may be verified that saying of Petrarch:

Virtu contro al Furore,
Prendera l'arme, e fia il combatter corto:
Che l'antico valore
Negli italici cuor non e ancor morto.
Virtue against fury shall advance the fight,
And it i' th' combat soon shall put to flight:
For the old Roman valor is not dead,
Nor in th' Italians' breasts extinguished.

Edward Dacre, 1640.

Chapter XXVI

Leadership Trait #26
Confidence—
Ability to Honor Yourself Whatever the Outcome

Machiavelli opens this chapter by creating a picture of the trouble that Italy was in at the time that he wrote this treatise. He suggests that the challenges that besiege Italy were beckoning in a new prince. He praises the current leader, Giuliano de Medici, stating, "Nor is there to be seen at present one in whom she can pace more hope than in your illustrious house with its valor and fortune . . ." He continues by stating that ideally you need to be prepared with your own forces as a firm foundation, whom would work much better as a team commanded, honored and financed by you. He then shares the weaknesses in Italy's opponents (the Spaniards cannot resist cavalry and the Switzers are afraid of infantry in close combat). Thus he suggests creating a new army—one that will resist cavalry and will not fear infantry. To end this final chapter of the book, he proclaims the words of Edward Dacre, 1640: *"Virtue against fury shall advance the fight, And it i' th' combat soon shall put to flight: For the old Roman valor is not dead, Nor in th' Italians' breasts extinguished."*

Confidence—the ability to honor yourself whatever the outcome is the leadership trait affiliated with the final chapter of this book. The greatest test of confidence is self-appreciation in the moment of defeat. Many leaders can fall, but those who are remembered and revered are the leaders who got back up again and continued on their crusades. The true test of your leadership abilities is how you kindly and compassionately you handle yourself when defeat is imminent.

1. Are there any areas of your life (in your business, religious, cultural, neighborhood or other) where leadership has failed and is seeking new direction? If so, list them.

2. Machiavelli suggests that preparation and a dedicated army that you manage, honor and finance sets you in a superior position for any potential battles that may ensue. In what ways are you prepared for challenges that could come your way?

3. In what areas and in what ways could you become better prepared? How? List the action steps or strategies you need to follow.

4. Machiavelli suggests a new army. Are there members of your team that would ideally be replaced? If so, list them.

5. What is holding you back from replacing these individuals?

6. What steps do you need to take to find effective replacements for them?

7. Who might you ask to join your team? Why?

8. If you could have anyone in the world join your team, who would they be and why?

9. What is preventing you from approaching the most ideal candidates for your team?

10. If you are need of better team members, create an action plan to recruit them, including deadlines. Then follow

through on the plan to ensure you have a winning team working with you.

11. The leadership trait affiliated with this chapter is *confidence—the ability to honor yourself whatever the outcome.* After having completed most of this manual, you should have a better indication of your progress. On a scale from one to ten (one being "not at all" and ten being "a great deal"), rate how confident you feel about yourself:

1——2——3——4——5——6——7——8——9——10

12. Make a list of the areas in which you currently lack confidence.

13. Reflect on each year of your life and write a list of all of the personal and professional accomplishments you have achieved.

14. Write a list of all of the challenges you have faced in your life.

15. How do you respond to the challenges? Are you proud of your performance?

16. On a scale from one to ten (one being "not at all" and ten being "a great deal"), rate how critical you are of yourself:

1——2——3——4——5——6——7——8——9——10

17. Are you harder on yourself than you are on others? If so, why?

18. What steps do you need to take to honor yourself and your achievements more?

19. What steps do you need to take to support and care more for yourself?

20. Write a "self-acknowledgment" pledge for yourself. Read it each day for at least the next month. Note any shifts in your actions or attitude in response to doing so.

21. Write a letter of gratitude to yourself for all of the efforts you have made throughout your life. Be sure to list your achievements in it. Then read the letter aloud to yourself on a daily basis.